# The Bible
# REEXAMINED

Eve
is
a hero.

Mary
is
not
a virgin.

Jesus
is
not
the way.

Randall Tremba

Author of *80 Dispatches from the Devil's Domain*
and *Let Love Arise*

Published by Four Seasons Press
114 W. German Street
Shepherdstown, WV 25443
304.876.3486

fourseasonsbooks.com

*The Bible Reexamined* is a must-read for those who live on the bridge between history and hope, facing the reality of humanity and trying to bring meaning to it. Tremba tells us with wit and wisdom that because of Eve, "humanity no longer lives in darkness, no longer stumbles along blindly."

— **Edgell Franklin Pyles, PhD**, Senior Chaplain Emeritus, Snowmass Chapel, CO, and author of *MAPS for Men: A Guide for Fathers and Sons*

Cherished beliefs are questioned and expanded upon in this thought-provoking collection of scriptural insights, but the questions can stretch and strengthen the reader's faith, even as it is reshaped.

— **Dr. Suzanne Shipley,** President Emerita, Shepherd University and Midwestern State University, Fulbright Scholar of the Holocaust

Wonderfully surprising, an intellectual pleasure, this book says what most of us don't know. To read it is to experience the melding of education and excitement.

— **Philip Bufithis,** author of the critical study *Norman Mailer*

With the acerbic wit reminiscent of Mark Twain, Tremba (who sort of looks like Mark Twain) cuts to the chase regarding the Bible's imperfect yet compelling message of love. By rescuing the Bible from both the lofty pedestal and the dusty trashcan, Tremba presents a "guide for the perplexed."

— **Bill Brown,** William Marcellus McPheeters Professor of Old Testament, Columbia Theological Seminary

Tremba, a Christianly-inspired humanist, guides us through a spate of revisionary convictions, e.g., the Bible is an insightful collection of texts written by people rather than THE WORD OF GOD, and "love, not Jesus, is the way." Readers who question their own Christian upbringings will find here a spirited and stimulating journey.

— **Douglas F. Ottati, PhD,** Craig Family Distinguished Professor of Reformed Theology and Justice, Davidson College

Page after page captures the nub of popular parables with wisdom, humor, and humanism distilled from the author's dynamic talents and transforming service as pastor, scholar, and community leader. The perfect book for anyone wrestling with what to do about all the mysteries, contradictions, and atrocities in, about, and behind the Bible.

— **The Reverend Patricia Donohoe,** author of
*The Printer's Kiss: The Life and Letters of a Civil War Newspaperman and His Family*

Tremba makes a compelling case for the place of the Bible in our lives. He approaches the Bible as a "human product," which allows readers all along the continuum of faith vs. reason to appreciate its truths—truths that are valid whether or not the Almighty wrote the text.

— **Stephen Altman,** author of the verse novel *Blues for the Muse* and the western novel *Bowhunter*

Tremba hits home on two key points that make the current theocratic trend both ironic and unjust: the Bible is manifestly a human book, written by ordinary humans within the limits of their own ancient context, not the declarations of an omniscient mind; and traditional interpretations and translations of the Bible simply get many things wrong.

— **Eric Thompson,** Professor Emeritus of Religion and Humanities,
Santa Rosa Junior College, and author of *Sourcery:
The History of Satan with Fresh Readings of Primary Sources*

To evangelicals and atheists alike, Tremba offers an understanding of the Bible that transcends literalism—or any "ism"—and embraces common cause. Like any important family meeting, this book may be uncomfortable for those with hardened views, but Tremba hosts with respect, humor, and love as he invites: "People, we need to talk."

— **Nathaniel "Than" Hitt, PhD,** Senior Scientist, West Virginia Rivers Coalition

*The Bible Reexamined* makes a compelling case that we have been misreading the Bible. Tremba is a thoughtful and expert guide to the history, subtext, and wisdom contained in this compendium. With references to Darwin, Springsteen, and other nontheologians, Tremba helps make both testaments seem new again. If you want a good book to explain the so-called "Good Book" this is the one.

— **Mark Madison, PhD,** Historian, US Fish and Wildlife Service,
National Conservation Training Center, Shepherdstown, WV

Whether you are comforted or confounded by the Bible, this is a refreshing and delightful must-read takes readers on a fantastic, revelatory journey through these ancient stories that forged our nation's past and loom large over our spiritual and political present.

— **Mary Anne Hitt,** Presbyterian ruling elder, climate leader and
contributor to the climate anthologies *All We Can Save* and *Not Too Late*

Thinking of Eve as a hero is certainly a novel idea. She "opened the door to insatiable curiosity." *The Bible Reexamined* is filled with these thought-provoking ideas. Readers with a sense of humor will appreciate the wit that can be found throughout the book.

— **Dr. David L. Dunlop**, President Emeritus, Shepherd University,
educator, author, and administrator

Tremba places the gospel story in the context of Old Testament prophecy. And in the Resurrection story, Tremba brings it all back home. The Way of Jesus is the Way of Love.

— **Stewart Acuff,** poet, union organizer, and author of *Playing Bigger Than You Are,
Justice Is Our Love in Action* and *Love Is Solidarity in Action.*

# Contents

# Dedication

## Ernest Barnwell Johnson Jr.
## June 26, 1930–August 16, 2021

Why Ernest? Here's why.

🍎 🍎 🍎

**Ernest Questions**
(From my blog, *The Devil's Gift*, September 12, 2021)

My friend died suddenly last month. He was 91. I was shocked and saddened. I also felt guilty. I felt as if I'd let him down. I'd known him as an acquaintance for 30 years, and then early last year we became friends.

My friend was born and raised in Alabama. His ancestors were Presbyterian, but his father married an Anglican and so my friend was raised Episcopalian. He went to Harvard and soon found the church and Christianity unpalatable.

He became a diplomat with the State Department. His assignments took him to many overseas countries. He developed an ecumenical outlook on all things religious.

Anglicans in Alabama are not Bible-thumpers. Nearly everybody else down that way is. The Bible is iconic in the South. Whether you believe it or not, you can't get away from it.

Two years ago my friend realized he had some nagging questions about the Bible. He called me.

(I mean, really, who ya gonna call? Jimmy Swaggart?)

Is this a crisis of faith? I asked.

*No, not at all. I'm just so damn curious about everything, and that includes the Bible. How in the hell did it become the Word of God?*

Good question. Short answer: It's not.

My friend came to my house.

*I know Moses didn't write the first five books of the Bible. So who did?*

No one knows. But we do know that it was composed, redacted, and compiled by many hands over a long time. And we know that each of the authors was blinkered. We know things they didn't. The Bible is a human product.

*I thought so!*

A lot of stuff in there is just plain wrong (the world was not created in seven days) not to mention immoral (holy wars, condemnation of homosexuality, subordination of woman, to name just a few). It's a bony fish. Good idea to pull out the bones before swallowing any of it.

*I agree!*

Actually, it's not even a single book. It's a collection of diverse works. We might think of it as we would a collection of Roman and Greek literary works. We can take the Bible into account, if we'd like, but we certainly don't have to be bound by it.

*You should put that into a book!*

Well, Ernest, I'm working on one right now.

*Hurry up. I'm old. I want to read it before I die.*

# Acknowledgments

No book springs full-grown from the head of Zeus or from any other head, including mine. Books are conceived, incubated, and delivered within a community.

My mother and father, Kate and Michael Tremba, taught me to respect the Bible before I could read. It was handled reverently during our family devotions. They revered it more than anything on earth, including the American flag.

My mother encouraged me to read one chapter from the Old Testament book of Proverbs every day (there are 30 chapters) and then start over each month. That will make you wise, she said. My father rose before sunrise every morning so he could read from his well-worn, extensively annotated Bible before catching the bus to his job with the P&LE Railroad.

At Wheaton College and Fuller Seminary I sat under the biblical instructions of Phil Hook, George Ladd, Daniel Fuller, and David Hubbard, to name just a few from those renowned evangelical institutions. From them and others I learned to appreciate the historic and cultural context of the Bible.

For 42 years I served the Shepherdstown (WV) Presbyterian Church. The members of the congregation were eager to learn. I never hesitated to share my latest biblical discoveries or questions with them. They were hungry for knowledge, and it encouraged me to press on and dig deeper. I owe them a deep debt of gratitude for their unwavering support.

I want to thank the Reverend Patricia Donohoe and Ethel Hornbeck, my colleagues in ministry at SPC. Pat helped me appreciate the artful beauty of scripture without overlooking certain ugly and despicable parts. Ethel opened my eyes to the mystical aspects of the Bible and ecumenical spirituality that I hadn't noticed before. Thank you, Pat and Ethel.

Following my retirement in 2017, I was asked to teach a course in the Lifelong Learning program at Shepherd University. Much of this book was developed and tested with a class of eager students. I am grateful to Karen Rice and Shepherd University for providing me that opportunity.

I've never nestled a baby in a womb, but I've heard a lot about it from my wife. Of course, nothing compares to bearing a child, but bearing a book in one's heart and mind comes pretty close. I was blessed with a savvy midwifery team.

For several years "The Confab" met over dinner once a month. Steve Altman, Bill Howard, Ed Zahniser, and Phil Bufithis repeatedly asked me: *How's the book coming?* They never let me forget that they and others actually expected a book from my hands someday.

Twelve years ago I met Dr. Jack Berkeley, a clinical psychologist. We became friends and met over lunch regularly. Every time the subject of my book came up he let me know he had no (as in zero) interest in the Bible, but he admired my passion for the subject. So, he kept asking: *How's the book coming along?* That too kept me going.

I want to thank the people who read an early, very rough draft of my manuscript. I needed to know if anyone other than I was interested in my project. Each and everyone of them said, *Keep at it.* So I did. They are: Stephen Altman, Patricia Donohoe, Leigh Koonce, Rie Wilson, Doug Thomson, Karen Thomson, Doug Utigard, and Ed Zahniser.

Rie Wilson also proofread the final draft before publication. She spotted numerous snags that the rest of us missed. Thank you, Rie!

A special thanks to Dr. Amy-Jill Levine, professor of New Testament and Jewish Studies at Hartford International University for Religion and Peace, who critiqued my next-to-final draft and offered many constructive suggestions.

I want to thank Lee Doty for introducing me to Natalie Kimber, a literary agent, who graciously helped me construct a succinct book proposal for potential publishers and, more important, helped me see the advantages of self-publication.

I want to thank my friends and colleagues who wrote pre-publication blurbs to endorse my work for potential publishing houses and as recommendations to potential readers.

I want to thank Tom Taylor for the concept, design, and layout of the covers for this book. I also want to thank the design team at HBP (Hagerstown, Maryland), especially Lori Schulman, for their enthusiastic support and creative work in designing this book.

And finally, my two incomparable and indefatigable editors.

Philip Bufithis, emeritus professor of English of Shepherd University and author of the critical study *Norman Mailer,* read and reread every line on every page of four different drafts. He kindly, yet pointedly, critiqued the case I was making in each and every chapter. Although he disagreed with some of my interpretations, he nonetheless helped make them stronger. We wrangled like two Talmudic rabbis, yet it was all in good fun. Phil's companionship on this journey was invaluable.

Elizabeth "Libby" Howard, a longtime copy editor for various prestigious magazines, did the line and copy editing for each and every draft, meticulously examining every sentence. Of course, I thought each draft was nearly perfect when I submitted it. She graciously showed me how it wasn't and how sentences and paragraphs could be improved, without hurting my feelings. I can't image anyone better at this work than she is. She sees things eagles miss.

Not only did Libby edit this book, she edited every essay I wrote for the *Good News Paper* for thirty-some years as well as all of my posts for *The Devil's Gift* blog for the past five years. I wouldn't be half the writer I am without her. I can't thank her enough. But I'll die trying.

Finally, I want to thank my wife, Paula, for coaxing me on when I got discouraged, which was often. She gave me time and space to work and think and pull my hair out.

# Glossary

**atheism:** disbelief or lack of belief in the existence of God or gods

**deism:** belief in the existence of a supreme being, specifically a creator who does not intervene in the universe; also an intellectual movement of the seventeenth and eighteenth centuries that accepted the existence of a creator on the basis of reason, but rejected belief in a supernatural deity who interacts with humankind

**evangelicalism:** tradition within Protestant Christianity emphasizing the supreme authority of the Bible, personal conversion, and the doctrine of salvation by faith in Jesus's death as substitutionary atonement for sin

**fundamentalism:** form of religion, especially Islam or Protestant Christianity, that upholds belief in the strict, literal interpretation of scripture; the Christian form is associated with reaction against social and political liberalism and with the rejection of the theory of evolution

**monolatry:** adherence to one particular god out of several, especially by a family, tribe, or other group

**humanism:** outlook or system of thought attaching prime importance to human rather than divine or supernatural matters; stresses the potential value and goodness of human beings, emphasizes common human needs, and seeks solely rational ways of solving human problems

**monotheism:** belief that there is only one god

**pantheism:** belief that the divine, nature, and the universe are one and the same

**polytheism:** belief in or worship of more than one god

**theism:** belief in the existence of a god or gods, especially in one god as creator of the universe, intervening in it and sustaining a personal relationship with it and its people

# Notes

## Capitalization

The word *god* is capitalized when it's associated with one of the three monotheistic religions—Judaism, Christianity, and Islam. In that context it is considered a proper noun: God. In most other contexts, *god* is considered a common noun. Some contexts may be ambiguous.

## Bible Translation

Unless otherwise noted, all citations are from the New Revised Standard Version. (The National Council of Churches, 1989)

## Names for the Two Parts of the Bible

The Old Testament is sometimes referred to as the Hebrew scriptures or First Testament. Judaism designates the collection as Tanakh—an acronym derived from TNK, the first letters of the Old Testament's three divisions: Torah (law/instructions), Nev'im (prophets), Ketuvim (writings). The New Testament is sometimes referred to as the Christian scriptures or the Second Testament. In this book I mainly use the traditional designations (Old Testament and New Testament), but not consistently.

## Dates

All dates are CE (Common Era) unless otherwise marked as BCE (Before the Common Era); *ca.* is short for *circa* which means "approximately."

## Alert

I was a preacher for forty-five years so you may come across some sermonizing here and there. I just can't help myself.

# Prelude

On June 1, 2020, following the removal of Black Lives Matter protesters from Lafayette Square across from the White House, President Donald Trump strode with an entourage of White House staff and military personnel to the front of St. John's Episcopal Church for a photo op. He displayed a Bible high above his right shoulder.

Many Americans wondered what that was all about. It was perplexing. Troublesome. Weird.

It looked to me as though Trump wanted to show the nation the "scepter" of his sovereign power and/or to quell the violence manifested in Black Lives Matter demonstrations roiling the nation that very day. I thought perhaps he was trying to exorcise a demon possessing our land.

The Bible as talisman.

The president did not hold up the presidential seal. He did not hold up the Declaration of Independence, the Constitution, the Bill of Rights, or Lincoln's Second Inaugural address—all precious to Americans. He did not hold up the Quran, precious to Muslims. He did not hold up the Tanakh, precious to Jews. He did not hold up a crucifix, precious to Catholics. He held up a Bible, supremely precious to evangelical Christians as THE WORD OF GOD.

That incident tells you all you need to know about the sway the Bible holds in American society. It has exceptional clout.

It shouldn't. But it does.

*The Bible Reexamined* aims to remove the Bible from its pedestal. It may be a good book, but it is not THE WORD OF GOD. Many Jews and Christians believe it is, but I don't. I will tell you why I don't and also why it's not as bad as some of you might think. The Bible belongs on the table with other ancient works. We may take it into account if we'd like, but we are not bound by it.

It's a bony fish. We mustn't swallow it whole.

# Introduction

The Bible has been on my mind for at least seventy-five years and on my desk for fifty. I was weaned on it. I read it daily. I studied it in college and seminary in its original languages (Hebrew and Greek). I exegeted it. I argued and quarreled over it with fundamentalists, evangelicals, agnostics, and atheists. I preached more than two thousand sermons from it over forty-five years.

I kept it on a pedestal.

I now know it's not what I once thought it was. It is not THE WORD OF GOD. It is far from perfect as literature or as an exemplar of morality. Still, it remains extraordinary among ancient works. I'd call parts of it divine as I do other human works.

I'd call certain works of Michelangelo, Bach, Shakespeare, Emily Dickinson, Alice Walker, China Achebe, or Arundhati Roy *divine*. That doesn't mean God *composed* their works. It means their work *evokes sublime feelings* that transcend rational explanation. It's like saying: *What a day! It's simply divine!* Even an atheist wouldn't quibble with that. Divine, after all, is both generic and particular. It all depends on the context.

Once I took the Bible off the pedestal, I saw it for what it is— flawed, tedious, mundane, boring, and yet engaging, edifying, and inspiring in places. It's not a novel, but it covers similar territory— nobility and treachery, courage and cowardice, compassion and cruelty, integrity and hypocrisy.

I no longer revere the Bible, but I do respect it, as I do my flawed parents. Respecting the Bible is not the same as worshiping it. Worshiping the Bible is bibliolatry, a form of idolatry prohibited by the Bible itself.

This book is a report on what I discovered after I removed the Bible from its pedestal, set it on a table, and read it as a human product. In the process I restored my love for it. As it turns out, I've had a stormy love affair with the Bible for a very long time. Under my breath I've been muttering: "I wish I could quit you, but I can't."

So, you might say, this is a love story.

🍎 🍎 🍎

My parents were fundamentalists. To them the Bible was THE WORD OF GOD, and belief in Jesus—or Christianity—was the only way to be saved from hell and attain eternal life in heaven. They often quoted John 14.6: *I am the way, the truth, and the life. No one comes to the Father but by me.* That meant (to them and many others) that Jesus was the only ticket to heaven. Believe it or perish! (Later I will show a completely different way to interpret that verse.)

As a child I uncritically absorbed the beliefs of my parents, who got their beliefs from certain preachers and teachers, who got their beliefs from an early twentieth-century movement known as fundamentalism, which itself derives from nineteenth-century millennialism. In other words, fundamentalism is a young version of Christianity compared with older and deeper traditions such as Catholic, Orthodox, Lutheran, and Reformed. At that time, I didn't realize how shallow, reactionary, and eccentric fundamentalism was.

Fundamentalists believe that every single word of the Bible was dictated by God as if to a stenographer. That's known as *verbal plenary inspiration.* Every word and syllable inspired by the Holy Spirit. That makes the Bible inerrant and infallible. Every word is factually and historically true. That's called *hard literalism.*

Evangelicals believe that God inspired the authors of the Bible while allowing freedom of treatment and literary style. (Bad grammar, misspelled words, and sloppy similes are on the writer, not on God.) That's called *soft literalism,* which means the Bible is not inerrant in matters of history, physics, or astronomy; but it is considered infallible in matters of faith and salvation, that is, "spiritual things."

For fundamentalists and evangelicals, the Bible alone contains the plan of eternal salvation, namely, how to get to heaven when you die. There is no other valid or reliable source of knowledge in that regard. The Bible is it!

Reason cannot show the way. Nature cannot show the way. No other book can. Only the Bible can.

For much of my life, that's what I believed.

I went along.

Eventually, I asked questions. I questioned both hard and soft literalism. I questioned the supernatural origins of the Bible. I wasn't ready to discard the Bible. It had been too much a part of my life. So I wrestled with it. I could no longer blithely overlook its contradictions and inconsistencies.

A careful reader can't help but see that certain stories contradict natural laws and scientific knowledge—for example, the creation of the world in six twenty-four-hour days (Genesis 1), Joshua making the sun stop "moving" for hours (Joshua 10.12–15), Elijah reviving the dead son of a widow (II Kings 17.22–22), Jesus walking on water (Matthew 14.22–33), and Paul reviving a dead boy (Acts 20.7–12).

The Bible also contains internal contradictions—for example, humans were created *after* the animals in Genesis 1 versus arriving *before* the animals in Genesis 2; "no one has seen God" (1 John 4.12) versus "Moses spoke with God face to face" (Exodus 33.11); "the women left the tomb and told the disciples" (Matthew 28.8) versus "the women left the tomb and told no one" (Mark 16.8).

Additionally and more tellingly, the Bible includes divinely sanctioned practices that are morally deplorable—condemning homosexuality, condoning slavery, authorizing genocidal holy wars, and endorsing the subordination of women. Such things have prompted many to toss the Bible into the trash can. But, to be fair, many ancient works contain reprehensible morality, sensibilities, and values according to our present standards.

For forty-five some years I had tried to soften offensive biblical passages. I could spin a troublesome or irksome passage. I had a few exegetical and semantical tricks up my pulpit gown sleeve. But trickery can take you only so far before you feel like a fraud.

As I continued reading and studying, I began to see another way to read the Bible. I didn't have to defend the Bible as THE WORD OF GOD, as something unique, infallible, and inerrant. I could treasure it for what it is: an anthology of works from a distant culture reflecting human struggles with perennial questions, issues, and problems. Consequently, I no longer hesitate to say the Bible simply got certain things terribly wrong. Even though they might have been acceptable in that time and place, they no longer are.

I came to see the Bible as a human product.

We can approach the Bible as a collection of ancient writings from Hebrew and Christian communities—the way we would approach a collection of ancient Greek and Roman or ancient Chinese and Indian writings. We don't need to handle it with kid gloves or bow before it. We can judge it by the same standards we apply to other works. And if we do, we just might find gems of wisdom in it, as we do in *The Way of Tao*, the *Bhagavad Gita*, *Hamlet*, *Middlemarch*, and *Jonathan Livingston Seagull*. If we are open-minded, epiphanies await us in all manner of literature, art, and music—including the Bible.

🍎 🍎 🍎

I left the church in June 2017. I thought I was just retiring, but as it turns out, I left the church in more ways than one.

After forty-two years of serving the Shepherdstown Presbyterian Church, I was glad that the congregation I left behind was strong, vigorous, and kind-hearted. I'm proud to have had a hand in cultivating a community with a reputation for courage, compassion, creativity, social justice, and hospitality. I'm grateful that garden is still growing and thriving to this day.

"Don't you miss it?"

Yes, I do. I miss the people. I miss the children. I miss my coworkers. I miss the music. I miss the tilling, weeding, and harvesting. But I don't miss the god that came with the turf—the anthropomorphic god of the Bible who intervenes in human affairs and sometimes doesn't, a god who saves some and damns others. That's theism, and it's in play in the following anecdote.

A woman cultivated her garden day after day, year after year. Her pious neighbor noticed how lush her garden was. One day he called out: "The Lord sure has blessed you with a beautiful garden!" The gardener replied, "Well, you should have seen it when the Lord was tending it on his own!"

The gardener didn't expect God to make her garden or the world a better place. The neighbor apparently did.

I'm with the gardener. A god that intervenes in the world here and there to make life pleasant for some and unpleasant for others just doesn't make sense to me anymore.

I've left that god behind.

And I'm pretty sure that's the kind of god Jesus left behind in the third temptation. "Jump and God will save you!" taunted the devilish Trickster as Jesus stood on a high precipice. "God will save you! It says so in the Bible. Psalm 91, verses 9 through 12 to be exact!"

(Yes, the Devil quotes the Bible.)

> *Because you have made the Lord your refuge,*
> *the Most High your dwelling place,*
> *no evil shall befall you,*
> *no scourge come near your tent.*
> *For he will command his angels concerning you*
> *to guard you in all your ways.*
>
> *On their hands they will bear you up,*
> *so that you will not dash your foot against a stone.*

"No, thank you," replied Jesus in so many words. "I don't believe in that kind of god."

Neither do I. I left that particular god behind. But I didn't leave Jesus behind.

🍎 🍎 🍎

I can't make you appreciate or respect the Bible, but I can (I think) remove some intellectual barriers, some jagged bones, so you can take it up and read it with appreciation for what it is. In this book I convey what I learned by reading the Bible as a human product. My perspective has been influenced by many others—some from long ago (Baruch Spinoza, Thomas Jefferson, Thomas Paine), who also approached it as I do. They, too, disregarded the supernaturalistic framing to better see the picture therein. To them and others, I am deeply indebted.

I invite you to trek with me across old terrain the way the renowned nineteenth-century English naturalist Charles Darwin (1809–82) explored old terrain and countless species with a fresh and unorthodox perspective. Darwin wanted to see and understand the world as it was, not as others said it was.

His approach inspired my approach to the Bible. Here is the result of that exploration.

THE BIBLE REEXAMINED: Eve Is a Hero, Mary Is Not a Virgin, Jesus Is Not the Way.

CHAPTER 1

# From Theism to Humanism

*I think that the absence of God can be really beautiful. It means it's our responsibility to take care of each other on this earth. And everything courageous and beautiful that we do is on us. And so I see my atheism very much as an act of optimism, that it is our job to make this world as good of a place as possible for as many people as possible.*

> — Vanessa Zoltan, former humanist chaplain
> at Harvard University, who says of herself:
> "I am a Jew, an atheist, and a humanist."

🍎 🍎 🍎

To be an atheist doesn't mean you deny divinity. It just means you don't believe divinity is male, narcissistic, sadistic, petty, or in one place.

There are other definitions of God, including one mentioned by the apostle Paul: *God is the one in whom we live and move and have our being.* (Acts 17.28)

And that just happens to be very close to the seventeenth-century Jewish philosopher Baruch Spinoza's idea of God. Spinoza (1632–77) was excommunicated for "not believing in God." But as it turns out, he did believe in God—just not the biblical theistic kind. He believed God was nature. He was a pantheist, not an atheist.

Spinoza was also a humanist. He believed in reason. He didn't blame God for plagues or earthquakes. He also believed that there was something greater to the world than the sum of its material parts. Something transcendental, mysterious, and awesome. Spinoza was a rational mystic.

He was raised by his Portuguese-Jewish family in the Netherlands where his ideas and works were published. And maybe that's why nearly half the Christians in the Netherlands today identify as "Christian atheists." Jesus without God.

To be sure, the Bible is overwhelmingly theistic. A personable, parent-like God is the primary protagonist. Even so, its theism is challenged from within the Bible itself. For example, the books of Ecclesiastes (life is random, without meaning) and Esther (no mention of divinity at all) deviate from the theistic paradigm.

What if theism is only a phase in human intellectual development and maturation? It easily could be. After all, the increase and enhancement of knowledge, wisdom, ideas, and understanding over time is obvious. Ideas, beliefs, and cultures evolve.

I once heard a rabbi on a podcast assert that the trajectory of the Hebrew scriptures begins in theism and ends in humanism.

(Tell me more!)

The narrative, he said, begins in Exodus with a man (Moses) liberating the Israelites from tyranny in Egypt with the aid of a supernatural power (God) and ends in Esther with a woman (Esther) liberating the Jews from tyranny in Persia with her own ingenuity and resources, without any aid from a supernatural power. In fact, the word *God* does not appear—not even once—in the Hebrew version of the book of Esther.

Was the author of Esther a budding humanist or an atheist? Who knows. But clearly the depiction of God evolves in the Old Testament. There's a trend.

At first the biblical God is just one among many gods. That's polytheism. Later God is proclaimed supreme above other gods: "You shall have no other gods *before* me!" That's monolatry. And later still, God is the one and only—all other gods are false, illusionary, mere idols. That's monotheism.

And that's a trend. From many to one. What's next? What's less than one? Some Jews (and others) would eventually say, "None."

Might that be called "progressive enlightenment?"

Of course, monotheism is famously uncompromising, exclusive, intolerant when it comes to other gods. But Judaism itself, far more than Christianity, has been quite accommodating to all kinds of ideas, including pantheism, atheism, socialism, and secular humanism. Perhaps that's because God in the Hebrew tradition is a verb, not a noun.

Make no graven images. Let God evolve.

And that brings us to one of my favorite stories in the Hebrew Bible—Moses and the burning bush. (Exodus 3.1–15. See appendix for full text.)

*Moses said to God, "If I come to the Israelites and say to them, the God of your ancestors has sent me to you, and they ask me, What is his name? what shall I say to them?"*

*God said to Moses, "I am who I am. [YHWH] Thus you shall say to the Israelites, I am [YHWH] has sent me to you. Thus you shall say to the Israelites, The Lord, the God of your ancestors, the God of Abraham, the God of Isaac, and the God of Jacob, has sent me to you: This is my name forever, and this my title for all generations."* (Exodus 3.13–15)

🍎 🍎 🍎

In the fictionalized world of Exodus, Moses had once lived in Pharaoh's palace as an adopted son. As you might recall, Pharaoh's daughter found baby Moses in a basket floating among the bulrushes in a stream where she had gone to bathe. She brought the baby home. Moses became a prince.

The young princess unwittingly selected Moses's birth mother, Jochebed, to nurse and raise him. We can imagine that by day Moses attended training classes for princes. And at night, his mother told him about his origins, about his rescue, about his adoption, about his native people, about Abraham and Sarah, Isaac, Ishmael, Esau, about Jacob and Rachel and their beloved son Joseph.

She told him about Joseph's brothers betraying Joseph and selling him to slave traders who took him to Egypt where he flourished and rose to power and how his strategic plan saved millions of lives during an extensive famine.

She told him how his ancestors had moved en masse to Egypt to be with Joseph. And she told Moses about the eventual enslavement of his people after Joseph died and was forgotten by succeeding pharaohs.

When Moses was born, the Hebrews had been enslaved in Egypt for four hundred years. Pharaoh intended to keep them (and other peoples) in bondage.

As Moses grew up and moved about the land, he witnessed the brutal treatment of the Hebrew people. He saw. He plotted. He struck. He killed a guard who was viciously beating an enslaved Hebrew.

Moses thought he would be a hero to his people. But no; the Hebrews and the Egyptians both turned against him. Pharaoh issued a death warrant. Moses panicked, fled Egypt, and settled far away in the desert land of Midian. He became a shepherd, married Zipporah, and had children.

Still, Moses did not forget his people. He agonized over their plight as many exiled leaders do. He remembered their suffering. His anger simmered. That low burn inside would not burn up until one day it burst forth, crying out to him from a burning bush.

Moses was tending his father-in-law's sheep in the high desert around Mount Horeb in the Sinai Peninsula when he saw a dry bush suddenly burst into flame, but not burn up. It just kept burning. Moses crept closer. A voice spoke from the bush.

*I have heard my people crying out in Egypt. I want you to deliver them from their oppression!* (Exodus 3.7–10, condensed)

(From a psychological point of view, the fiery bush could be a projection of an "unquenchable fire" in Moses's own heart, namely, a burning desire to free his people who were suffering under Pharaoh's whip in Egypt.)

"Strange," Moses must have thought. "The God of my ancestors has heard what's been burning in my ears all these years."

*I want you to go down to Egypt and deliver my people from bondage.*

(God's desire and Moses's desire were one and the same. Strange. Strange, indeed.)

Who, me?

*Yes, you.*

Once Moses gained his footing, he asked for God's name because Pharaoh would surely require credentials, a credible and respected sponsor, before allowing a *nobody* an audience before the throne.

"What is your name?"

And that's when Moses discovered that the name of the God of his ancestors (Abraham, Isaac, and Jacob) is a verb, not a noun. *"My name is YHWH,"* which happens to be the Hebrew verb *to be* ("I am who I am" or "I will be what I will be").

YHWH.

I AM.

Which is to say, God is *being*, not *a* being.

I AM.

(That name was so holy that ultimately no devout Jew would say "Yahweh" out loud. I'm pretty sure "Do not take the Lord's name in vain" was meant to prohibit shallow, sanctimonious, and mindless repetitions which cheapen the holy.)

I AM.

Moses pocketed that name and went down to Egypt. He stood before Pharaoh and was asked by what name or authority he presented himself? Moses replied (using YHWH as the name for his god): *I am who I am.*

Yes, this is a serious story, but I find it a little bit humorous that Moses basically says to the mightiest ruler on the planet:

*I am who I am. Deal with it!*

And therein lie the seeds of humanism.

*I am who I am.*

(Say it once! Say it loud!)

Of course, it's only an inkling of humanism because Moses would rely on a theistic god to intervene with a series of ten plagues inflicted on Egypt while Pharaoh dithered over whether to free the slaves.

*I say to you: Let my people go!* (Exodus 5.1)

God as a verb, of course, is not the only way Judaism depicted God. But it is one way. Apparently, some of the Hebrew prophets and mystics intuited that ultimately God can't be defined, contained, constrained. (Or, we might say: A god that can be defined is no god at all, by definition.) And maybe that's why making a graven image of God is forbidden in Judaism. After all, a solidified golden calf (or solidified verbal images, such as dogmas or creeds) cannot evolve. It's lifeless.

So here in the Bible itself is a latent corrective to dogmatic theology: "I will be what I will be." Or in the vernacular: "What I was, or what I am, is not necessarily what I will be. Don't fence me in. A pox on all your calcified theologies!"

It's hard for most of us to think of God without some kind of image in mind, although many Jews and Muslims can manage. It's a cliché but true: *We make gods in our own image.* As the Greek philosopher Xenophanes (560 BCE) put it: "If horses could draw, their gods would look like horses."

Better to have no image in mind, but if we make gods in our image, we can unmake them.

Remember that although both the Jewish and Christian traditions are rooted in biblical texts, neither is restricted by or confined to the text. Each community's theology evolved beyond the text into new meanings, interpretations, and understandings of the divine. In other words, there's more to Judaism and Christianity than just the Bible. Both are living and evolving traditions.

Still for most Protestants in Europe for a long, long time, God was unquestionably the theistic God of the Bible however perceived or misconstrued. In the nineteenth century, however, that God was publicly weighed in the balance and found wanting. Yes, Biblical theism had made sense of the world for many people for nearly three thousand years. But not so much anymore. Humanism began to make more sense for more and more people whether they identified as humanists or not.

But, just to be clear, theism or humanism or any other -*ism* without compassion is defective, a noisy gong or a clanging cymbal. As Shakespeare put it: "Sound and fury, signifying nothing."

Hollow.

The gradual replacement of the theistic paradigm by the humanistic paradigm has been going on since at least the eighteenth century through the works of Immanuel Kant, David Hume, Thomas Paine, Voltaire, Friedrich Nietzsche, Mary Wollstonecraft, Denis Diderot, and others. In fact, centuries before the Common Era, Greek philosophers such as Socrates, Plato, Protagorus, and Lucretius challenged the validity of gods for explaining natural phenomena. As Protagorus (460–420 BCE) put it: "Man is the measure of all things." And that, too, is a seed of humanism.

Humanism is now ascendant. To paraphrase the Israeli humanist Yuval Noah Harari from his book *Homo Deus: A History of Tomorrow* (2016): Fewer people than ever blame God for famines, earthquakes, diseases, tsunamis, poverty, and suffering. Nor do most people expect God to deliver the world from such calamities and maladies. Many people, perhaps even most, now look to science to identify causes of calamities and to develop solutions for eliminating or mitigating them.

In my view, the "miraculous works" of Jesus can be seen in the work of agronomists, epidemiologists, and therapists who are saving millions of people from hunger, disease, and mental anguish with new knowledge and new tools. Jesus can be seen as a model of human capacity for compassion and care.

The Jesus of the gospels—whether historical, fictional, or a combination—inspires and emboldens courage and compassion in countless people. That's why I did not leave Jesus behind. That's why I'm a Christian humanist, matriculating in the "school of love," a lifelong learning program.

I put a lot of faith in science and the scientific method. But I do not believe the scientific method is the only path to knowledge and understanding. Poets, prophets, and artists from all times and places, including from within the Bible, reveal truth and wisdom science alone can't.

# CHAPTER 2

# What Is the Bible?

*Question with boldness even the existence of a god because, if there be one, he must more approve of the homage of reason than that of blindfolded fear. You will naturally examine first the religion of your own country. Read the Bible then, as you would read Livy or Tacitus.*

— Thomas Jefferson, from a letter to his nephew

🍎 🍎 🍎

*Read the Bible. It will scare the hell out of you.* (Bumper sticker)

Indeed! The Bible has scared many. It contains bloodbaths, beheadings, assassinations, incest, rape, torture, and monsters seeking human prey. All of which, of course, you can see in *Game of Thrones*.

If you like *Game of Thrones*, you'll love the Bible.

Okay, that may be a stretch. Millions watch *Games of Thrones* as sheer entertainment. Billions read the Bible as THE WORD OF GOD.

In this and the following chapter I aim to dethrone the Bible as THE WORD OF GOD. I see no reason to make more of it than it is. The Bible is a human product.

🍎 🍎 🍎

The Old Testament is a collection of writings from the ancient Hebrew people. It includes stories of their mythic origins, legendary founders, renowned figures, and momentous events. These works also include heroic feats, cowardly deeds, insurrections, civil wars, disease, famine, conquest, immigration issues, border conflicts, marriage regulations, inheritance laws, critiques of the wealthy elite, health and dietary codes, and royal court intrigues, plus a gallery of poets, prophets, martyrs, humane rulers, tyrants, swindlers, war criminals, and would-be messiahs.

The Bible is similar to texts other nations have assembled or could assemble. The United States, for example, has its revered "scriptures"—the Declaration of Independence, the Constitution, the Bill of Rights, Washington's "Farewell Address," Lincoln's "Second Inaugural Address," and an assortment of other documents—plus legendary figures (George Washington, Daniel Boone, Paul Bunyan, Davy Crockett, Harriet Tubman, Abraham Lincoln, Carrie Nation, Teddy Roosevelt) and an origin myth (the Pilgrims and indigenous peoples sharing a feast at Plymouth).

As it turns out, the Bible itself is an unofficial founding document of the United States. Seventeenth-century English and Dutch migrants to North America referred to *their* new land as a New Israel. They considered it their "Promised Land" in keeping with their "exodus" from "Pharaohs" in the Old World. Consequently, these new arrivals viewed the indigenous peoples (Indians) as the biblical "Canaanites."

*But as for the towns of these peoples that the Lord your God is giving you as an inheritance, you must not let anything that breathes remain alive. Indeed, you shall annihilate them—the Hittites and the Amorites, the Canaanites and the Perizzites, the Hivites and the Jebusites—just as the Lord your God has commanded, so that they may not teach you to do all the abhorrent things that they do for their gods and you thus sin against the Lord your God.* (Deuteronomy 20.16–18)

The Pilgrims and Puritans had read their Bibles and they believed it sanctioned their conquest since they were also "the chosen people of God." (Dutch Reformed Boers also cited the Bible to justify their conquest and domination of southern Africa in the eighteenth century.) The settlers couldn't help themselves. They felt anointed, empowered, and sanctified by THE WORD OF GOD.

It should be noted, however, that the Old Testament contains laws regulating and constraining conduct in war. (*When you go to attack a city, you must first offer peace to the people there.* Deuteronomy 20.10) Furthermore, the God of the Old Testament—

though typically regarded as a warrior—is also portrayed as merciful. (*The Lord, a God merciful and gracious, slow to anger, and abounding in steadfast love and faithfulness, keeping steadfast love for the thousandth generation, forgiving iniquity and transgression and sin.* Exodus 34.6–7). The God of the Old Testament is both stern and merciful. In other words, like us. After all "we make gods in our own image."

John Winthrop (1587–1649), a Puritan lawyer and governor of the Massachusetts Bay Colony, heralded America as a "city on a hill," echoing language from the Sermon on the Mount. (Matthew 5.14) America, he said, was to be a beacon of morality and virtue for the world, just as Israel—God's *other* chosen, *other* exceptional people—was to be. And, indeed, among the ancient peoples, Israel's law, moral code, and prophetic voices were exemplary.

Strangely, despite the Puritans's reference to Jesus's Sermon on the Mount ("city on a hill"), Jesus was not their model. Moses and Joshua were. Moses, the lawgiver, and Joshua, the conqueror, were cited by preachers frequently in America's early days. In other words, the Old Testament provided a founding narrative for the United States. Benjamin Franklin even suggested that Moses be represented on the national seal. Not a bad idea since Moses advocated love of neighbor, hospitality toward migrants, care of widows and orphans, as well as *just* courts.

(Representing Joshua would have been a bad idea.)

The Bible played a large role in the founding of the United States. From the seventeenth through the nineteenth centuries, the Bible was cited repeatedly in public discourse and debate. Not surprisingly, to this day biblicists and secularists thrust and parry in many public debates, each seeking to constrain or dominate the other. One cites special revelation; the other cites reason.

🍎 🍎 🍎

The Bible (from the Latin, *biblia,* book) may be similar to other religious books and collections from other peoples, but, we can't overlook one consequential fact: It, unlike any other book, has been extolled by billions of people as THE WORD OF GOD.

How did one particular book become THE WORD OF GOD?

I will address that question in the next chapter. I'd like to begin with another, simpler question: How did a collection of assorted works become *the Bible?*

The Bible looks like any other book—pages between two covers. But it was not always in that form. Furthermore, it is not an organically unified work like most books. It's an anthology of sundry documents loosely related to each other. It's a conglomeration.

The books of the Bible were initially scrolls—parchment spooled around two wooden poles. The book format (known as a codex) was invented in the fifth century CE. I don't know but I can imagine that many people were unsettled and upset by books replacing scrolls, the way people today are unsettled by digital readers replacing physical books. I once heard someone say that devotees of scrolls thought the pages of a book chopped up the continuous flow of an unfolding, rolling narrative. Books sliced and diced.

And yet books won out.

Scribes gradually converted scrolls into books. Thus, an assortment of scrolls was assembled into an assortment of books. (By the way, these books were not divided by chapters and verses initially. Numbered chapters were inserted in the thirteenth century and verses in the sixteenth century.) Original drafts were edited and reedited. Consequently, each manuscript has its own history of production similar to the process of making books or movies these days.

(The letters in the New Testament are an exception. Paul likely wrote or dictated at least some of his letters but still most of them are composites. Of the thirteen letters attributed to Paul, most scholars consider only seven as authentic, that is, from his hand or dictation.)

Certain Old Testament books were woven together from separate documents. It's not apparent to the untrained eye, but scholars have ways of recognizing "stitch lines," as, for example, in the five books of Moses (the Pentateuch)—Genesis, Exodus, Leviticus, Numbers, and Deuteronomy. Scholars now know that multiple documents known as P, J, E, D (for Priestly, Jahwist, Elohist, Deuteronomist) were merged into final versions hundreds of years after Moses's lifetime. After all, his death is narrated in Deuteronomy 32.50.

Eventually those five scrolls were designated as Torah, traditionally called "the books of Moses," even though Moses is not the author.

Isn't that fraudulent?

No. Not in that culture.

It was customary in the ancient world for an author or authors of a manuscript to attribute their work to a venerable person. Unlike writers today, writers in antiquity did not have copyright or profits in mind. Furthermore, attributing a text to a venerable person venerated the text as well.

Solomon is credited for the Song of Solomon, which he likely did not write. David is credited for many psalms, which he likely did not compose. The prophet Isaiah gets credit for composing chapters 56–66 of Isaiah, which his disciples (the school of Isaiah) most likely wrote.

The production of most biblical manuscripts was like editing the raw footage of a film today, a filmmaking step many people know nothing about. And yet an editor's role in shaping a movie is as critical as that of the screenwriter and the cinematographer. The cohesiveness of the final product is the result of editing. Editing is both a craft and an art. It's creative. The books of the Bible were edited. And redacted.

One who splices together film segments—pacing and organizing a movie—is called a film editor. One who splices together various textual segments is called a redactor. Most Old Testament books were redacted. The redactors are unknown.

As Stephen Greenblatt put it in *The Rise and Fall of Adam and Eve: The Story That Created Us*, "The Torah as a whole, most scholars agree, was first redacted in the fifth century BCE. One or more editors took multiple strands that had reached them from the past, compared them, corrected them, cut pieces from them, added pieces to them, adjusted them, reconciled them to the best of their abilities, and wove them together."

Of course, we would love to see the original drafts (the director's cut) or the final drafts in their original form. But the original documents have been lost. Instead, we have copies made from copies. But the same is true of the works of Homer, Plato, Lucretius, Virgil, and Tacitus. We possess only copies of copies of their works. And it should be noted, far fewer of those exist than copies of biblical manuscripts. Greek and Roman manuscripts didn't have the benefit of an extensive network of monasteries staffed by thousands of devout copyists. Each copy has a pedigree and chain of custody.

Determining the authenticity of copies was one thing. Determining which of the multitude of sacred books in circulation would be included in the official canons of the Old and New Testament was something else.

Why were some works included and others excluded?

The formation of both canons was a ragged development. We know that Jewish elders in the sixth century BCE and Christian bishops in the second century CE began assembling and collating their respective sacred writings.

Some scholars think the Old Testament canon was established in the second century BCE during the Hasmonean dynasty (ca. 140–37 BCE). Others think it was not until the third century or even later. The canonization of the Hebrew scriptures was a fluid process over five or more centuries.

The New Testament canon was formed more quickly, but it still took more than three centuries to finalize. Partial listings of the Christian scriptures appear in letters from bishops in the mid-second century. The complete list of all twenty-seven, however, appeared for the first time in a letter composed by Bishop Athanasius of Alexandria in 367 CE.

Again, the formation of each canon was fluid over a long time.

Furthermore, no one entirely knows the criteria used for inclusion in either canon. We know that several Old Testament books (Ecclesiastes, Song of Solomon, Esther) and several New Testament books (Hebrews, James, Second Peter, Second and Third John, and Revelation) were accepted belatedly, after much debate. Moreover, books such as Tobit, First and Second Maccabees, the Gospel of Peter, the Epistle of Barnabas, and the Didache were acknowledged by many as inspired scripture, but were considered apocryphal and thus excluded from certain Hebrew and certain Christian canons.

Despite the bumpy and contentious process of canon formation, the Council of Rome (382 CE) officially defined the books to be included in the canon implying its formation as guided by the Holy Spirit—distinct and unique from any other collection of ancient works. It was placed on a pedestal.

Even today many Christians aver a supernatural hand directing the formation of the biblical canon. "It's not an arbitrary, politically determined collection," fundamentalists and many evangelicals would say. "It's the work of the Holy Spirit. So don't question it! The Bible is THE WORD OF GOD from start to finish. Period." As Eric Davis, founding pastor (2008) of Cornerstone Church in Wyoming put it:

*So, what council determined what would be in the Bible? Because of God's act of inspiration, the only council which determined what would be in the canon and what would not, was the counsel of God. God inspired the canon by his Holy Spirit. In God's providence, regenerate man recognizes the canon by the illumination of the Holy Spirit.*

But as the exercise below will show, there is a natural explanation for the formation of the canon. The exercise will also show by way of analogy how strange, astounding, incredible, and dangerous it is to claim that the biblical canon is THE WORD OF GOD.

🍎 🍎 🍎

Imagine you're part of a class assigned to compile a list (a canon) of a hundred important American books or a hundred important films. Such a collection would be similar to the collection known as the Old Testament, the national literature of the ancient Jewish people. The New Testament, though not a "national" collection, is a conglomeration of texts from a Jewish sect.

Imagine the questions you'd ask and the decisions you'd face.

After much wrangling the project is complete—a hundred books bound into one volume or a hundred films compressed onto one DVD. (Probably not practical, but then we're pretending.) You call them The Book or The Movie.

What if this canon of American books or films was distributed worldwide? How would readers and viewers in China, India, Kenya, or Bolivia understand each particular work? What would be lost in translation?

(Although some Jews and some Greeks still read the Bible in its original languages, most people read translations.)

Would non-Americans understand nuances? Would they understand the iconic status of 1776, July Fourth, April 15, 9/11, Lexington, Valley Forge, Gettysburg, Antietam, Pearl Harbor, Hiroshima, Smokey the Bear, Mickey Mouse, Uncle Sam, or January 6, to name just a few notable names and dates that might appear in the canon? In most places July 4 is just a date. In the United States it's packed with emotion.

(Ancient Israel had its own lexicon of symbolic names and numbers familiar to them but unfamiliar to us.)

Would readers and viewers recognize different genres? Would they know the differences among the Declaration of Independence, the Constitution, *The Federalist Papers, Common Sense, Walden, The Scarlet Letter, Leaves of Grass, The Cat in the Hat*, or *The Handmaid's Tale?* Would viewers from other societies know the differences among *The Sound of Music, Wall-E, Schindler's List, Blazing Saddles, Titanic, La La Land, Dunkirk, Star Wars, Pulp Fiction, Avatar, Barbie*, and *Lincoln*?

(The books of the Bible are not of one genre.)

Now imagine that after a century or two, the United States government proclaimed those canons as THE WORD OF GOD—the one and only infallible source of knowledge, morality, jurisprudence, and truth for the whole world? What if people were punished or tortured for saying it wasn't?

Huh?

Well, that's pretty much what happened with the Bible.

# CHAPTER 3

# The Bible Weaponized

For nearly fifteen hundred years Christians revered and treasured the Bible as a primary source of truth and moral guidance. Church officials cited it in support of doctrines, polity, spiritual practices, and liturgical rites. The Bible was venerated, but it wasn't worshiped. It was not the only or final authority on all matters. The rules, regulations, and decisions of the pope, bishops, and church councils were also taken into account. Authority was multipolar.

That is, until the sixteenth century and the Reformation.

In the sixteenth century the Bible was hailed as THE WORD OF GOD. The battle cry of the Reformation was *sola scriptura*—the Bible alone as the source of essential knowledge, doctrine, and practice. Its authority would supersede popes and sovereigns.

Coincidentally, in that same century verse numbers were inserted into every chapter of the Bible. Thus, religious opponents were able to parry "chapter and verse" back and forth to win arguments.

Why did the Bible become THE WORD OF GOD in the eyes of millions and millions of people?

Short answer: The sixteenth-century reformers elevated it to ultimate supremacy as a counter to the authority of the pope and the Roman Church counsels. It became the indispensable sword and shield for the Reformation.

Why did the Reformers do that? Short answer: A brewing religious and political rebellion needed a credible moral authority.

According to a Protestant view of the situation and conditions (Catholics see it much differently), German ruling princes resented papal agents who sold fraudulent indulgences (grants from the pope to reduce time spent in purgatory) and extracted heavy taxes from their subjects to build an extravagant cathedral in Rome. The general population resented taxes as well. Many felt the way some Americans feel toward the federal government: "They're taking my hard-earned money for self-aggrandizing projects."

Resentments simmered.

The masses—living in grinding poverty—also resented the luxurious lifestyles of popes and bishops. "The one percent" prospered; the rest struggled.

Resentments boiled.

Furthermore, the Church required works of piety (prayer, penance, pilgrimages) of already beleaguered parishioners. If they didn't comply with the rules, they were told, their souls were in danger of eternal damnation. People lived in fear of hell.

(By the way, Christianity did not invent the idea of hell. Notions of unpleasant destinations for the less-than-virtuous were common in ancient societies. But those places were relatively benign and nebulous, like the Hebrew Sheol and the Greek Hades. It took the medieval Church—with graphics provided by Dante's *Inferno*—to transfigure hell into a physical place of endless fiendish torture and torment in eternal flames with no escape. Hell was weaponized and monetized. The idea of heaven and hell as binary eternal destinations pervaded Western cultures. It became a mental fixture, a metaphysical geography for religious and nonreligious alike. Real or not, heaven and hell are powerful images in religion, art, poetry, and humor.)

Through a vast pedagogical and propagandistic campaign, the Church had convinced people that hell was very, very real. People desperately wanted to be "saved" from that. "Please tell me what I must do to be saved! I'll do whatever it takes!"

We may think that silly because the afterlife is merely speculative to many of us. For many, this life is real and may very well be all the life we get. So we'll pay most anything—exorbitant prices for pharmaceuticals, surgery, medical devices, and health insurance.

Whatever it takes to prevent, eliminate, or reduce physical misery and extend our physical life as long as possible.

Previous generations paid bishops and priests for prayers, relics, and indulgences to save their souls. But by the sixteenth century people were questioning the validity of certain remedies and the veracity of certain promoters.

*Where do these requirements come from? Are they valid? Are they baseless? Just made up? Could we be victims of misinformation and malpractice? Have we been hoodwinked?*

We have similar questions regarding modern diagnoses and remedies.

*Is our natural fear of death and dying being exploited? Are they making up new things to scare us and make us submit to their expertise? Have we been had?*

The sixteenth-century reformers thought the Church exploited people. Martin Luther, John Calvin, Menno Simon, Zwingli, and others challenged church dogmas and practices. The reformers were determined to purge the Roman Church of corruption, extravagance, and superstition and return it to its original, simpler foundation.

(Of course, we can suspect mixed motives within the reformers. Underneath the sanctimonious slogans was, in part as always, a desire for control and power.)

Still, to conduct an insurgency, the reformers (labeled Protestants, from *protesters,* by their Catholic opponents) needed an authority by which to adjudicate their claims against the supreme authority of church councils and popes. After all, the Roman Church dominated nearly all territories, states, and even kings and emperors.

But who or what could stand against indisputable authority? What authority could the reformers cite or claim? Their own voices were not enough. They needed something common folk would accept as a legitimate counterauthority.

Similarly, the American Revolution needed a counterauthority to the British monarchy. When the patriots rebelled against

King George in 1776, they cited "self-evident truths" from the English philosopher John Locke (1632–1704). For many, that was legitimate and convincing. It was enough. It gave them something to stand on against monarchy.

But self-evident truth was not an option in sixteenth-century Europe. It was unheard of. Yet nearly everyone had heard of the Bible, even if they hadn't read it.

Well, what about the Bible?

Yes, what about the Bible, indeed. The Bible was a plausible candidate as a counterauthority. It had been proclaimed as a higher authority by other dissenters such as John Wycliffe and Jan Huss in the fourteenth century and William Tyndale in the fifteenth century. And they had paid a high price. They were excommunicated, exiled, or burned at the stake. Many surmised that if the Bible evoked such fear, it must be a potential rival to Church authority.

And it was.

The reformers bet the ranch on the Reformation. They bet the Reformation on the Bible. Henceforth, said the reformers, truth must be verified by the Bible, not by church councils or popes. It would be their sword and shield.

After all, Martin Luther had discovered his revolutionary idea in the Bible. *Therefore, since we are justified by faith, we have peace with God through our Lord Jesus Christ, through whom we have obtained access to this grace in which we stand; and we boast in our hope of sharing the glory of God.* (Romans 5.1–2)

In a flash Luther saw that faith *and only faith* mattered, not works of piety. The Church did not teach or support that idea, he declared. The Church promoted works of piety for salvation. Thus, according to Luther, the Church was in error.

Serious error. Or so he claimed.

It should be noted that Luther cherry-picked from the Bible to suit his own agenda and perhaps some psychological crisis as well. (See *Young Man Luther: A Study in Psychoanalysis and History* by the psychologist, Erik Erickson.) Luther ignored the part of the Bible that says: *Faith without works is dead.* (James 2.26) He insisted that faith alone (*sola fides*) assured one's eternal salvation. "Faith alone" and "Scripture alone" became battle cries against the Roman Church.

The reformers frequently quoted the apostle Paul: *All scripture is given by inspiration of God, and is profitable for doctrine, for reproof, for correction, for instruction in righteousness that the man of God may be perfect, thoroughly furnished unto all good works.* (2 Timothy 3.16–17)

And that (*all scripture is given by inspiration of God*), the reformers reasoned, means that the Bible is infallible, unlike fallible popes and their minions. Thus, the Bible was put on a pedestal. It became the "paper pope."

And therein lies a major problem.

Unlike the audible voice of the actual pope, the "paper pope" can't speak. It has no heart, no brain, and no vocal cords. It can't reply to questions. Someone must speak on its behalf, despite the bumper sticker:

*The Bible says it. I believe it. That settles it!*

Of course the Bible may "speak" to a reader the way an Emily Dickinson poem may "speak" to a reader. That's different. That's personal. It's not public.

The Bible "says" nothing. Instead, fallible and flawed people tell us what the Bible says and what we must do to conform to its imperatives. They pepper their admonitions with "Thus sayeth the LORD" or "the Bible says" and manage to cajole many. They pick and choose from the Bible's thirty-three thousand verses, amplifying some while suppressing or ignoring others.

So as it turns out, people put their faith in certain preachers and interpreters, not in the Bible itself. Scripture is once removed. Between the believer and the Bible stands the expounder. Thus, scripture alone (*sola scriptura*) is not sufficient. An interpreter is necessary.

Whom can we trust?

No one can know everything about everything, so we all must trust somebody in certain matters. For example, I know next to nothing about auto mechanics. Therefore, I have to trust somebody else to fix my car. Not every mechanic is competent or honest. I've been duped. It takes some searching to find a good one—one I can trust.

If the Bible is important to you, you should be at least as careful in finding a trustworthy spiritual mentor or biblical expositor as you are in finding a trustworthy auto mechanic, plumber, or primary physician. Of course, why we trust one person more than another is largely subjective, but it doesn't have to be irrational.

The Reformers trusted themselves more than the Roman Church authorities. They also trusted ordinary people—up to a point. They encouraged people to read the Bible for themselves, but with a caveat: They insisted that readers rely not merely on their own ability but also on the aid of the Bible's supernatural author, the Holy Spirit. Whatever that was, it was a caution against too much self-confidence.

The Reformers might put it like this: "You don't need a priest or bishop to tell you what the Bible says. You can read it for yourself. But also pray that the Holy Spirit will enlighten your mind." Consequently, ecclesiastical authority was bypassed. That was a cultural and political milestone. A paradigm shift. A radical idea.

Anglican church authorities looked askance at it. They felt threatened. They demanded submission to their authority just as King George demanded submission to his rule. Ironically, and tragically, Puritan church officials in Massachusetts would also demand submission and suppress religious freedom. (Those who displace authoritarian power often replace it with their own. It's an old story.) Thus, Roger Williams fled and founded Providence in Rhode Island as a haven for religious dissidents

The idea of individual personal authority became a primary factor in empowering common people to rebel against the Church of England's bishops and, by extension, the English king. And that led to this: *We the people!* The people—you and me (well, we men)—are sovereign. No pope, no bishop, no king will rule over us!

Individualism flourished, in part, because the Reformation cultivated self-confidence by putting the Bible directly in the hands of common people. (For a thorough analysis of that phenomenon, see the evangelical historian Mark Noll's work *America's Book: The Rise and Decline of a Bible Civilization, 1794–1911*.)

Coincidentally, the opportunity to possess a Bible only became practical in the sixteenth century because of Gutenberg's printing press. It made the Bible widely available and affordable. Like the internet in our day, the printing press radically changed accessibility to information. More and more people could hold the supreme authority, the Bible, in their hands. Literally.

The Bible was cocked and loaded in the hands of thousands of people. Open-carry was encouraged. A compact New Testament could fit in a shirt pocket like a derringer. It was only a matter of learning how to wield it.

Luther knew how to wield it. He became a hero following his trial (called a Diet) by the Holy Roman Emperor at Worms on the Rhine River in 1521 where he exclaimed: "Since then your serene majesty and your lordships seek a simple answer, I will give it. Unless I am convinced by the testimony of the Scriptures or by clear reason (for I do not trust either in the pope or in councils alone, since it is well known that they have often erred and contradicted themselves), I am bound by the Scriptures I have quoted and my conscience is captive to the Word of God. I cannot and I will not retract anything, since it is neither safe nor right to go against conscience."

In that moment Luther singlehandedly absolutized the Bible and the individual's conscience over against any other authority. The Bible became a fixation for Protestants.

During my high school days, I often cited the Bible in religious arguments with my Catholic friends. They never retorted with Bible verses. It seemed like they barely knew it. In fact, they seemed to blithely dismiss it as irrelevant. Only much later did I figure out why. Their religious education was much broader than mine. Protestants, like me, were obsessed with and narrowly focused on the Bible as the one and only source of truth and morality. We were masters at wielding it.

My Catholic friends, on the other hand, were learning about the lives of saints, studying a comprehensive catechism, as well as receiving biblical instruction. The "Bible alone" was a Protestant thing. We were still weaponizing it against Catholics 500 years after the Reformation. Clearly Catholics had more things going for them, including a renaissance of biblical studies, scholarship, and publications as a result of Vatican II (1962–65).

🍎 🍎 🍎

In the wake of the Reformation, personal and private interpretations of the Bible flourished. Protestants became biblicists, dueling each other with chapter-and-verse barrages. The reformers had opened a can of worms. There was no longer a single, authoritative arbiter of biblical meaning. Disputes raged. Disparate churches and denominations united, multiplied, divided, reunited, and divided again and again.

(Imagine the United States without the Supreme Court to settle disputes about the Constitution. Imagine every citizen, town, or state as a "constitutional authority," doing whatever seems right in its own eyes, experts be damned.)

Who's to say what interpretation or application of the Bible is right or wrong, valid or invalid? In most cases, it doesn't really matter. But some interpretations can have dire consequences if implemented in public policy and practices.

In the United States evangelical leaders wielding their Bibles and their interpretations have had a particularly outsize influence on presidents and presidential policies and positions.

During Ronald Reagan's administration (1981–88), James Dobson, founder of *Focus on the Family* (a popular radio show that promoted patriarchy in families and denounced homosexuality), was a frequent adviser to the president. Reagan heard Dobson's Bible-based views on public policies. We don't know whether Reagan heeded any, but we know he heard them.

In March 2024 the evangelical TV preacher Hank Kunneman said of the criminal charges facing Donald Trump. "This is really a battle between good and evil. There's something on President Trump that the enemy fears: It's called The Anointing." (Reuters).

At a Trump rally the evangelical pastor Joel Tenney preceded his invocation with these words: "Be afraid. For rulers do not bear the sword for no reason. They are God's servants of wrath to bring punishment on the wrongdoer. And when Donald Trump becomes the 47th president of the United States, there will be retribution against all those who have promoted evil in this country."

With that, he invited the audience to remove their hats as he prayed. "Lord, help us make America great again." (The Atlantic, September 2024)

In other words, THE WORD OF GOD is on their side. And on Trump's side.

Okay, I know, it's a free country. And I don't begrudge ordinary individuals their personal biblical interpretations. Generally, they do no harm. But I do worry when Bible-toting, Bible-quoting evangelical leaders have ready access to the White House so they can assure the president that war, segregation, climate-change denial, homophobia, Islamophobia, or their "pro-life" agenda is right and righteous. Apparently, having sworn their oath of office on the Bible, presidents feel obligated to defer to THE WORD OF GOD. Or appear to do so to win the "evangelical vote."

Putting the Bible on a pedestal was a tragedy. The Protestant movement, particularly its fundamentalist and evangelical offshoots, gradually embedded the notion of the Bible's supremacy as THE WORD OF GOD in Western culture, especially in the United States. Nothing is more sacred in the Bible Belt. (Although the Confederate flag would be a close second.)

The Bible's dominance didn't just happen by chance or divine decree.

The hegemony of the Bible was accomplished through a relentless barrage of sermons, pamphlets, books, and Bible conferences and a constant stream of radio and television broadcasts. The evangelist Billy Graham preached to millions around the world, waving his Bible as "God's Word" in what were called "crusades." All these programs and projects were organized by communication-savvy people who sincerely believed they had the truth in a book and were ordained and obligated to bring it to "the lost."

Yes, these types of people are sincere. But sincerity is not enough. The *Peanuts* cartoon character Charlie Brown lost every baseball game he pitched. After every game he lamented, "How can I lose when I'm so sincere?"

Fundamentalists and evangelicals are sincere but blinkered about the nature and status of the Bible. Many of their interpretations and extrapolations from it are misconstrued and harmful. Sincerity is not enough. Charlie Brown was sincere but he was also a lousy pitcher.

As a result of sophisticated broadcasting and crusading, the Bible as THE WORD OF GOD took hold in American culture and other societies where Western missionaries spread THE WORD. Millions and millions of people came to believe that the Bible contains the one and only plan of salvation. Believe it or perish!

The persistence of those proselytizers makes some unbelievers think twice: Could the Bible actually be THE WORD OF GOD? Perhaps I should take Pascal's wager: *It's better to believe and be wrong than to not believe and be wrong.*

(Of course, what we believe isn't as rational as that wager implies. If only it were.)

# CHAPTER 4

# The Bible Scrutinized

In the wake of the Reformation, the Bible became a dominant force in the Western world. It inspired art, music, and literature. It informed governance, laws, and morality. Kings, queens, and emperors swore oaths on it. It was considered supernatural, inerrant, and infallible. It was put on a pedestal. For nearly four hundred years it was above criticism.

And then in the nineteenth century, something happened. German scholars—influenced by the eighteenth-century Enlightenment—questioned the Bible's supernatural origins. Others might have questioned it previously but now apt tools (manuscript dating, cultural anthropology, and philology) were available. Archaeologists focused on finding evidence to support the biblical narrative.

Biblical scholars investigated the formation of the Bible the way Darwin had investigated the formation of species in nature with apt tools and methods. In both cases, supernaturalism was disregarded. Only empirical, fact-based explanations were admitted. The "age of reason" was in full bloom. Skepticism was in vogue.

The Bible was off the pedestal and on the examination table. It was dissected line by line, not disdainfully, but out of respect. After all, to probe the history, techniques, and materials behind an artistic composition like Leonardo da Vinci's *Mona Lisa* is not disrespectful. Such attention honors the painting and the artist.

These scholars were in many cases believers, not infidels or scoffers. They were detectives probing a mystery, searching for clues, building a case. A single word could be revealing. Scholars found anachronistic words and names in the texts. They discovered that the stories of Moses, Joshua, David, and Elijah were composed hundreds of years after the purported time line.

Despite concerted efforts, hard evidence was lacking to support much of the Bible's reputed history. For example, no one found fragments of Noah's ark on the mountains of Ararat or of the walls that came tumbling down in the battle of Jericho. Biblical history, as it turns out, is *remembered and repackaged* history. It is not historical as we understand historical. It must be taken with a grain of salt.

That is not so unusual. Twenty-first-century American Christian nationalists repackaged eighteenth-century Thomas Jefferson as a Christian to support their claim that the founders intended the United States to be a Christian nation. That's just not true. Jefferson was a deist—not a theist. He was a secular humanist. He believed in reason, not revelation. He advocated separation of church and state, a democracy, not a theocracy.

(And just for the record: He enslaved people.)

*Repackaged* history often serves a certain agenda that may or may not be constructive or beneficial to all.

Biblical scholars also identified a variety of genres, including folktales and mythic poems in the Bible. Valid interpretations would have to take genre, not just words, into account. Genre matters. Nevertheless, many modern readers, focusing on empirical truth, miss what even premodern people understood intuitively. The Bible is an anthology of diverse genres, much as our hypothetical canon of American books or films would be.

As Karen Armstrong put it in *The Lost Art of Scripture: Rescuing the Sacred Texts* (2019): "Too many believers and nonbelievers alike now read these sacred texts in a doggedly literal manner that is quite different from the more inventive and mystical approach of premodern spirituality."

Biblical scholars concluded that the Bible was a human product, not divine. Their announcements and publications created shock waves. American professors imported these findings into American universities. Skepticism toward Christian verities became vogue, chic, radical. Students spoke of these new ideas to their parents, including fundamentalist and evangelical parents.

Alarm bells went off.

Fundamentalists and evangelical parents were horrified. They believed such ideas maliciously undermined the authority of the Bible. To probe and dissect biblical passages with the tools of empiricism was, to them, sacrilegious. The devil's work. Christianity was under attack. Apostasy threatened the churches and the nation.

Fundamentalists and evangelicals denounced universities and colleges as bastions of liberalism and godlessness. They accused faculty of teaching "pernicious" ideas and corrupting their children's faith. To remedy that travesty, they created alternative, safer institutions to protect their children.

(Not exactly "homeschooling" but the higher education equivalent.)

Evangelicals founded Christian liberal arts colleges such as Gordon, Wheaton, and Westmont while fundamentalists founded Bible institutes such as Moody and Biola so their children could live and learn in a "spiritually safe environment." Fundamentalists and evangelicals wanted the Bible affirmed as the infallible WORD OF GOD.

Period.

Through such evangelical institutions and an expanding media infrastructure (camps, conferences, magazines, radio, television), a fervent subculture grew within the larger American culture. At first it was only thousands, but it soon became millions. It pervaded nearly every Protestant denomination. The Bible as THE WORD OF GOD was its unifying theme. The Bible now had an army of zealous defenders.

I was one of its foot soldiers right through my high school days.

Although I respect the historical-cultural, critical approach to the Bible, I also realize that uncritical reading—even random reading— can touch and transform lives. And it has. After all, words in and of themselves are powerful. As Emily Dickinson put it, "I know nothing in the world that has as much power as a word." Sometimes a single word or sentence heard or read—even out of context—at the right time can turn a life around. It "speaks" to the hearer or reader.

Critical scholarship cannot dampen the feelings evoked by certain scriptures. "The Lord is my shepherd." (Psalm 23) "Where can I flee from your presence? If I ascend to the heavens, you are there; if I make my bed in the depths, you are there. If I rise on the wings of the dawn, if I settle on the far side of the sea, even there your hand will guide me, your right hand will hold me fast." (Psalm 139) "Love one another as I have loved you." (John 13.34) "Now faith, hope, and love abide. But the greatest of these is love." (1 Corinthians 13)

Despite what scholars may say to contextualize or demythologize the Bible, millions of people still love it—the Psalms, the prophets, the gospels—without reservation.

But love doesn't have to be blind.

One's appreciation of the Bible can benefit from and be enriched by scholarship.

Mine has.

One particular discovery reframed Genesis 1–11 for me.

# CHAPTER 5

# Genesis 1 as a Parable

Creationists wield the biblical story of creation to oppose the exclusive teaching of evolution in American public schools. Using the Bible to disparage the scientific theory of evolution is a reason many people dismiss the Bible as irrelevant and even harmful.

As Karen Armstrong put it in *The Lost Art of Scripture* (2019): "Because [the Bible's] creation myths do not concur with recent scientific discoveries, militant atheists have condemned the Bible as a pack of lies, while Christian fundamentalists have developed a 'creation science' claiming that the book of Genesis is scientifically sound. Not surprisingly, all this has given Scripture a bad name."

The polemical use of Genesis 1 stems from a singular fixation by fundamentalists on pitting it against the theory of evolution. As it turns out, it is not an alternative to, or a rival of, evolution. It's poetry, not exposition.

And that's a good thing. Evolution is based on empirical evidence. "Creation science" is not. In fact, most scientists view "creation science" as religion, not science.

Still, creationists demand that it be taught in public schools as an alternative to evolution. That, of course, alarms people who consider creationism as religious, and thus a way to surreptitiously inject Christianity or at least theism into the classroom and place religion and science on an equal footing.

They are not equal.

As "the Great Agnostic" Robert Ingersoll (1833–99) put it: "Teaching the biblical story of creation in a high school biology class should be as unthinkable as telling school children that thunder and lightning are produced by Thor's hammer."

Pitting the creation story against the theory of evolution is foolish and inappropriate. One account is poetic, the other empirical. They don't belong in the same debating forum.

Unfortunately, most people see Genesis 1 only in light of the 150-year-old debate. Consequently, their view of Genesis 1 has been prejudiced. They don't know that long before the creation-versus-evolution debate, Genesis 1 was seen by many as an allegory, not as historical fact. The current literal view of Genesis 1 is quite new and yet fixed in many people's minds as the *only* view.

Understandably, then, it is difficult for many people to see Genesis 1 as something other than a foil for evolution. It is not a foil for evolution. It's a beautiful poem open to many interpretations. Before I present reasons for seeing Genesis 1 as a parable, let's review the origins of the creation-versus-evolution debate.

Charles Darwin left the biblical God out of his explanation for the origin and formation of species. Darwin's naturalistic approach arose from an intellectual trend fostered by the eighteenth-century Enlightenment. Its guiding principles may be summarized like this:

*Question authority. Practice skepticism. Propose a theory and test it against the facts. Look for evidence. Measure things.*

Darwin did. Persistently. Religiously.

By leaving the supernatural out of his approach, Darwin could entertain the theory of natural selection. He realized that the geological ages and fossil strata that the English geologist Charles Lyell presented in *The Principles of Geology* (1830) undermined "young earth" datings, such as the popular date of 4004 BCE for the origin of earth. The earth was much, much older than that. What did that mean for biology? Darwin wondered.

Darwin collected and categorized multiple samples of flora and fauna. He analyzed the data and concluded that species with random mutations best suited for survival and reproduction became more prolific while species without such random mutations became less prolific. It wasn't necessary to invoke serial interventions by a supernatural being. Natural selection was sufficient.

Darwin's theory shocked his world. People gasped.

His theory left God out.

Even so, as details of natural processes were publicized, people came to see the world as more glorious, not less. Darwin's discoveries evoked awe and reverence without invoking God as the Creator.

And that was a problem.

The Bible explicitly depicts the natural world arising from the speech of God over six twenty-four-hour days. For nearly two thousand years in the Western world, the seven days of the creation story was largely accepted as true. Few questioned the veracity of Genesis 1.

Then along came Darwin.

In contrast to seven days, Darwin's theory required long spans of time—eons, billions of years—for the natural world to emerge. Few people could fathom that, let alone believe it.

In Darwin's time people in the West believed the earth was about six thousand years old. James Ussher (1581–1656), the Church of Ireland's Archbishop of Armagh and Primate of All Ireland, emphatically declared that the world was created in 4004 BCE on the twenty-second day of October at 6:00 p.m.—Greenwich time, I assume.

Ussher deduced that date by calculating the various genealogies and life spans of biblical characters listed in Genesis. His claim had credibility since it was based on the Bible (THE WORD OF GOD), not on dubious science. Even today, many fundamentalists believe 4004 BCE is the correct date for the earth's origin. In fact, that date is printed as an annotation alongside Genesis 1 in certain Bibles, as if that date itself is part of the biblical text, GOD'S WORD.

Eventually, some people questioned Ussher's date and method because a "young earth" didn't square with the physical data of fossil records coming to light. Darwin had empiricism on his side.

Ussher did not. Ussher's evidence was internal to the Bible. For a growing number of people influenced by the Enlightenment, that wasn't good enough. They wanted empirical evidence.

Still, most people believed the bishop's dating—in part because the masses accepted ecclesiastical answers to virtually everything. And in part because in the wake of the fourteenth-century Renaissance, nearly everyone assumed that ancient texts from Plato, Aristotle, Tacitus, for example, were the sources of all necessary truth. Scholars and clergy extrapolated truth from authoritative texts, including the Bible, of course. These lights from the past, it was thought, could illuminate the present better than anything modern or anything in nature.

Anything new was suspect.

The scientific method was new.

So when scientists such as Copernicus (1473–1543) or Darwin, claimed to have discovered "new truths," it was unsettling. It was what is voguishly called a "paradigm shift" (Thomas Kuhn's phrase from his 1962 book, *The Structure of Scientific Revolutions*). It takes time, often generations, to adjust to such a radical shift in perspective—for example, the earth revolving around the sun instead of vice versa. People were skeptical and scornful.

*Scientists must be crazy! Everyone can see the sun revolves around the earth. The sun comes up. The sun sets. And now scientists are claiming we descended from apes!*

New truths drove many minds off their rails. Many people adamantly resisted Darwin's claims. He not only challenged assumptions about the natural world, but even more disturbing, his theory undermined the veracity of the Bible, THE WORD OF GOD.

*If the Bible isn't true on its first page, what about the rest?*

In Darwin's day, most people in Europe trusted bishops, priests, and pastors more than scientists. Most Christians believed *and felt* that the Bible was THE WORD OF GOD and was therefore trustworthy.

Darwin's theories rattled their faith.

*If humans evolved from apes, what's left of the "image of God" in humankind? What happens to human dignity and the sanctity of life?*

Following the publication of Darwin's *On the Origin of Species* (1859) and *The Descent of Man* (1871), people took sides. Science or the Bible? Darwin or the Church? Evolution or creation? Pick your side. And remember: *Your soul is at stake.*

Throughout the nineteenth century and into the twentieth, the issue was hotly debated. Professors and preachers were shunned, shamed, or fired for being on the wrong side. And then in 1925 the debate landed in a state court in Dayton, Tennessee.

A high school teacher, John Scopes, had been recruited to test the ban on teaching evolution. He presented the theory in his classroom and then by previous arrangement, he was arrested and a trial was set.

The national media flocked to Dayton. The renowned defense attorney Clarence Darrow and the equally renowned prosecutor William Jennings Bryan went at it. The whole nation paid attention.

To be fair, Bryan worried more about the social implications of evolution than the biological aspect of it. He opposed social Darwinism—the idea that certain people become powerful in society because they are innately better, as in "the survival of the fittest." It should be noted that social Darwinism has been used to justify imperialism, racism, eugenics, and social inequality at various times over the past century and a half. By the early twentieth century social Darwinism had attracted many influential and even educated people. Today evolutionary biologists "unequivocally reject social Darwinism," according to the research biologist Nathaniel Hitt.

Still, Bryan aggressively pressed his case against Scopes, and the jury found him guilty. He was fined a token one hundred dollars and told to cease and desist. The trial ended, but the public debate did not. It continued in pulpits, on the radio, and in school boards.

Fundamentalists perceived the theory of evolution as an existential threat to their ultimate source of authority and, just as important, a challenge to the morality based on it. The "battle for the Bible" had begun. Fundamentalists went on the offense.

*To concede to evolution destroys the reliability of the Bible, discredits its God, and undermines its moral codes. We can't be good without God. We can't know God without the Bible.*

For fundamentalists Genesis 1 was a redline—to accept the legitimacy of evolution would be the first step on a slippery slope toward moral decay and disaster. It was more than an intellectual issue. They feared for their children's spiritual well-being and eternal salvation.

(Who doesn't want to protect their children from physical or spiritual harm—real or perceived?)

Alas, it was an unnecessary stance to take. There was nothing to fear if Genesis 1 had been seen for what it is—poetry, not exposition; a parable, not history. In fact, it is as benign and inspiring as the parable of the good Samaritan.

If fundamentalists had only known and appreciated the Bible's diverse literary forms rather than treating nearly all its contents as history, things might have turned out differently. But fundamentalists would not heed or even consider alternative interpretations and explications. They were paranoid, defensive, and stubborn. They didn't trust egghead "intellectuals." For them the Bible was literally true in every way and in every word. Period. They stood firm against critics and scoffers.

*The Bible says it. I believe it. That settles it.*

Unwittingly, fundamentalists imposed on the Bible a standard for truth—empirical verification—from the Enlightenment itself. That criterion for truth was unknown to biblical authors, who had a broader understanding of truth. Fundamentalists believe that because the Bible is THE WORD OF GOD, nothing in it can be false, incorrect, inconsistent, or contradictory. It is infallible and inerrant. "God cannot lie." Therefore, everything in it can be *verified* factually.

But empirical verification of propositional truths, as it turns out, is a fairly modern approach to the Bible.

Genesis 1, for example, wasn't always viewed as historical or factual. In his book *History of the Bible* (2019) John Barton tells of a second-century text known as the Epistle of Barnabas. The author alleges that Genesis 1 is not about the creation of the world but about the "new creation" that Christians experience in Christ. That's not a literal interpretation.

Church fathers, such as Origen in the second century and Bishop Augustine in the fourth century, considered Genesis 1 allegorical, not literal. The great Jewish scholar Moses Maimonides (1135–1204) insisted that nothing in the Bible, including Genesis 1, should be taken literally.

Genesis 1 can be and has been read as something other than literal. Sadly, fundamentalists seem unaware of venerable allegorical approaches to the Bible. To them, anything that looks remotely historical is factual.

So they set out to prove the historicity of the Bible—to rub its critics' noses in its facticity.

To support their claims, fundamentalists and evangelicals funded foundations that sent archaeologists to dig up proof, literally. If Noah's ark landed on the mountains of Ararat (Genesis 8.4), there must be physical traces of it. If the walls of Jericho fell at the blast of horns from Joshua's army (Joshua 6), there must be rubble at that site. If Solomon built the most glorious temple ever (1 Kings 6), there must be evidence buried under Jerusalem.

Dig, dig, and keep digging!

But such efforts are futile because many Old Testament stories are dubious history. Many of the stories and tales are embellished or embroidered—not to deceive but to inspire pride in Israel's glorious past; to arouse feelings, not to convey historical, unadorned facts. All nations create such stories to glorify and solidify certain national events and heroes as well as to entertain, inspire, and edify their people.

Sure, nonfiction can be powerful. But fiction can be powerful too. *Uncle Tom's Cabin* is fiction. And it moved a nation.

The story of creation is fiction. It's a parable. It can move people—as we will see.

As I see it, the creation story was published and recited during the Babylonian Exile (sixth century BCE) for one paramount reason: *to inspire and empower personal and national resolve for a people sorely discouraged.* The seven-day week is merely a poetic device for the poetic parable and prophetic message.

*Listen, my people. Let me tell you a story and you will see that we have power to rebuild our devastated lives. Once upon a time, a beautiful world arose out of chaos and darkness. It took hard work. But we can do that too.*

The parable of creation, like the parable of the good Samaritan (Luke 10.25–37), is fictional yet true. Let's take a look at that parable.

*An expert in the law stood up to test Jesus. "Teacher," he said, "what must I do to inherit eternal life?" He said to him, "What is written in the law? What do you read there?" He answered, "You shall love the Lord your God with all your heart and with all your soul and with all your strength and with all your mind and your neighbor as yourself." And he said to him, "You have given the right answer; do this, and you will live."*

*But wanting to vindicate himself, he asked Jesus, "And who is my neighbor?" Jesus replied, "A man was going down from Jerusalem to Jericho and fell into the hands of robbers, who stripped him, beat him, and took off, leaving him half dead. Now by chance a priest was going down that road, and when he saw him he passed by on the other side. So likewise a Levite, when he came to the place and saw him, passed by on the other side. But a Samaritan while traveling came upon him, and when he saw him he was moved with compassion. He went to him and bandaged his wounds, treating them with oil and wine. Then he put him on his own animal, brought him to an inn, and took care of him. The next day he took out two denarii, gave them to the innkeeper, and said, 'Take care of him, and when I come back I will repay you whatever more you spend.' Which of these three, do you think, was a neighbor to the man who fell into the hands of the* robbers?" He said, "The one who showed him mercy." Jesus said to him, "Go and do likewise."

ぎ ぎ ぎ

The good Samaritan story cannot be verified empirically, but—I think you will agree—it is true nonetheless. Even if the *facts* are unverifiable, the moral lesson is true: To "love your neighbor" means to care for all people, regardless of ethnic, racial, gender, or religious identity. The parable rings true to our feelings, intuitions, and aspirations. It inspires and edifies.

The good Samaritan story uses actual things and places in its fictional world, but the story itself is not factual.

Was Jesus lying?

No.

But what if someone or some group set out to prove that the story of the good Samaritan was indeed a historical fact in order to defend the inerrancy of the Bible? After all, it is THE WORD OF GOD, and God does not lie.

I think you'd agree that would be a waste of time and effort. Does it really matter whether an actual Jew was mugged on the Jericho Road on a certain day or whether two people or three people passed by without stopping, or whether a certain specific Samaritan stopped to offer aid?

*What was his name and age?*

It would be a waste of money to send archaeologists and forensic experts to scour that road and vicinity, to search for the names of the three villains or scrutinize guest registries from local inns.

*Exactly when and where did the Samaritan deliver that mauled Jewish man? And where was that inn located?*

Parables do not require historical verification or validation. They convey moral truth.

Again, pitting the story of creation against evolution is like putting a cactus and a cockapoo in a boxing ring. That's no match.

That's no fight. That's an exhibit. We can admire each thing separately without rejecting one or the other.

Yet for the past one hundred fifty years creation and evolution have been forced into a boxing ring. It's a shame. It's a tragedy. Because the story of creation in Genesis 1 can be heard as a parable of hope.

How we hear something—a song, poem, or story—often depends on our circumstances. Consider an example from our time.

Bruce Springsteen's song "My City of Ruins" (*Come on and rise up.*) was written about the degradation of his beloved Asbury Park in New Jersey. But when Springsteen sang that song on national television following the 9/11 attacks and then again in New Orleans after Hurricane Katrina in 2005, it was heard far differently. It empowered a nation and a city to rebuild. It gave us hope. It gave us resolve.

*We pray for the strength, Lord. We pray for the faith, Lord. Rise up. Come on. Rise up.*

The story of creation is one thing in a debate. And that's how most of us have heard it—as a polemic against evolution. But the story of creation is something else when you're feeling down and out, hopeless, with no direction home. It's no longer ancient cosmogony. It's a summons to re-create, to rebuild. It affirms and proclaims the human capacity for creative and transformative action.

*Come on, we can do this. We can transform chaos into order, darkness into light, death into life!*

Genesis 1 has been called a myth or mythic, but I prefer to call it a parable since parables convey a lesson or a message.

What is the message in the poetic parable of creation?

🍎 🍎 🍎

# CHAPTER 6

# Lessons from the Parable of Creation

*When God began to create the heavens and the earth, the earth was complete chaos, and darkness covered the face of the deep, while a wind from God swept over the face of the waters. Then God said, "Let there be light," and there was light.* (Genesis 1.1–2)

*Thus, the heavens and the earth were finished and all their multitude. On the sixth day God finished the work that he had done, and he rested on the seventh day from all the work that he had done. So God blessed the seventh day and hallowed it, because on it God rested from all the work that he had done in creation.* (Genesis 2.1–3. See appendix for full text.)

🍎 🍎 🍎

The Bible was not divided into chapters until the thirteenth century. Some divisions seem arbitrary or misplaced. For example, the story of the seven-day creation begins at Genesis 1.1 with the first day and ends with the seventh day at verse three in chapter 2. Hence, the complete reference for the seven-day creation story is Genesis chapter one, verse one, through chapter two, verse three. (Genesis 1.1–2.3) I will use "Genesis 1" as a shorthand for Genesis 1.1–2.3.

The parable of creation comes from a people well acquainted with suffering, one crushing defeat after another. Suffering brings wisdom. Or can. The ancient Hebrew people suffered. A lot. They gained wisdom. Deep wisdom.

In the sixth century BCE the Babylonians destroyed Jerusalem (Zion) and forcefully relocated much of the population of Judaea to Babylon (located in modern Iraq).

*By the rivers of Babylon we sat down and wept when we remembered Zion.* (Psalm 137)

They faced existential anxiety, a deep abyss. Despair. Darkness. Dread.

*Will we ever live and thrive again? Who or what will save us? Will the light ever dawn upon us again.*

And then along came a prophet-poet with a story of hope, a parable of creation in seven verses, framed as a single week. Once upon a time, order and beauty arose out of the abyss, out of chaos and darkness. And it can happen again.

Yes, Genesis 1 reads like cosmogony, an origin story, but that's incidental to the parable, just as the Jericho road is incidental to the good Samaritan parable. The pressing questions in exile were not cosmogonic.

*Hmmm . . . I wonder: How did the world begin? Where did the sun, moon, stars, plants, and animals come from? What came first? Who or what did it?*

Those are interesting questions, but for another time. In exile the urgent questions were: *How do we get out of this terrible mess? Can our world be repaired and rebuilt? Will God save us? If not, who or what will?*

(We, too, face those questions—more than once. *My world has collapsed! My head's under water. I can't breathe. What shall I do? What can I do? Who or what will save me?*)

In their hour of darkness, the Hebrew people needed something other than cosmogony. They needed something more than polemics against other origin stories. They didn't need information. They needed inspiration. And, as it turns out, what they heard in Genesis 1 was good news—gospel—long before the gospels of the New Testament appeared.

*You are not helpless. You are not doomed. You have the power to overcome suffering.*

That gospel is rooted in the meaning of "made in the image of God." We will get to that later in this chapter. But first let's ponder that seventh day (*And on the seventh day God rested*) before we return to day six with its announcement that humans are made in the image of God.

The day of rest is the apex of the parable. And that's no surprise because of all the Mosaic laws and practices, it is the fourth commandment ("Keep the Sabbath holy") more than any theological creed ("The Lord our God is one") that sustains Judaism. The Talmud (the body of Jewish civil and ceremonial law and legend) affirms the Sabbath's importance with lines such as these: *Destroy the Sabbath and you will destroy the Jewish people. More than Israel kept the Sabbath, the Sabbath kept Israel.*

Practice is worth a thousand creeds.

In the Talmud the Sabbath is referred to as a "bride" and a "queen." According to tradition it's a day for singing, dancing, reading poetry, and making love. Consequently, Sabbath is enshrined as the culmination of the creation narrative. The workweek ends with a day of joyful leisure and re-creation.

What a great and simple idea.

But questions arose.

What about doing this or that on the Sabbath? How far can I walk? How many sticks can I pick up? Can I light a lamp? What if my mule falls into a ditch?

Rabbis answered question after question. Rules, regulations, and exemptions were made and codified in order to assist people in knowing how to keep this most holy (and most healthy) of commandments. The array of rules and restrictions regarding the Sabbath indicate its importance for the Jewish people.

We must rest from our labors. And here's how.

We all need to take a break—regularly, religiously. Sabbath observance is healthy for mind, body, and spirit. It's healthy for families, communities, and societies. It's humane.

(By the way, rules and regulations are not necessarily odious. For example, we may agree that "all you need is love," but then wonder what love requires in this or that situation. After all, love is not merely affection. It's action. It's regard for another. It's complex. We need guidance. And that's why the Psalmist exclaimed—much to our surprise, perhaps—*The law is my delight.* (Psalm 119.174) Why? Because if you want to love God and love your neighbor with all your heart, you need some practical guidance on just how to do that. And the more we ask, the more examples and rules multiply.)

The fourth commandment is a gift to humanity. And so are its explications.

Humans can't live on bread alone. Nor can humans live on work alone. We need leisure. Purposeful rest allows the human in us to blossom.

Hence the seventh day is the ultimate scene in this parable. The end of our labor is joy. Or should be. The creation story did not invent the seven-day week. It employed it as a poetic device.

By the time of the Babylonian Exile, Sabbath observance had been a practice for centuries. Moses (whether historical, fictional, or a blend) didn't invent the seven-day week, but he may have invented the Sabbath. (Although given the inevitable cross-fertilization among societies, he could have appropriated it from another culture.)

Sabbath observance, Moses insisted, would enable his people to protect and preserve their humanity, dignity, and freedom. Otherwise, they might as well have remained slaves in Egypt, working relentlessly.

Yes, we can become slaves to work.

So the seventh day is no minor coda in this parable. The poet declares, perhaps humorously, that even God the Almighty, "who neither sleeps nor slumbers" (Psalm 121), needs a break from work.

*And on the seventh day God rested.*

And in that moment, time—and not just deeds and places—was made holy.

Moses believed that with hard work, former slaves could become masters of their fate. But if their drive to make things or to make the world better was relentless, then they'd be slaves to a goal, even if that goal was noble. Workaholics would contaminate and degrade their society. So everybody—no matter their social status—was granted (and mandated) a day of rest. Or else!

As a child I thought the intent of this commandment (*Six days SHALT THOU LABOR and do all thy work*) was to make people WORK because if left on their own, nobody—me, for example!—would want to work. Get to work or else! God said so.

I thought work was the mandate, not rest. But as it turns out, rest is the mandate. If you want to be "healthy, wealthy, and wise," incorporate rest into your routine and don't rely on spontaneity. Etch it on your calendar. Set a reminder alert. That's how a habit is formed—by willful repetition until it becomes second nature.

*Plan your work. Work your plan.*

*Plan your rest. Rest your plan.*

And now back to the sixth day, the penultimate scene of the creation parable. On that day humankind—male and female— emerges, "made in the image of God." (Genesis 1.27) Divinity is reflected in humanity, or so the poet says.

That brought comfort to the Hebrew people, as it does to many today. No matter what their Babylonian masters said or did to them, dignity was inherent in their nature.

*We are created in the image and likeness of God. And no one can take that away from us.*

But there's more to the designation ("image and likeness") than dignity. What might that be?

The meaning of the phrase is critical to understanding the lesson of the parable. We are animals, yes. But what do we possess that the other animals don't? How does the "image of God" in humans make them different?

Could it be immortality? Language? Imagination? Rationality? Artistry? Soul? Consciousness? Opposable thumbs? (Huh?) All those and more have been proposed as the meaning of "image of God."

But the answer is simple. The answer is right under our noses, though many have missed it.

*If humans are like God, what is God like?*

Look at the parable. Leave all other notions about God out of your answer. Set your theology aside. What does God do in *this* parable?

The answer: *God works.* God works methodically, creatively, and with purpose. "By the seventh day God had finished the *work* he had been doing; so on the seventh day he rested from all his *work*." (Genesis 2.2–3)

God worked persistently to transform darkness and chaos into something good, whole, wholesome, and beautiful. Light out of darkness, order out of chaos, abundance out of scarcity. And that means, according to this parable, that we have the capacity to do the same in our own world. We are capable of creative, transformative work.

And that's good news!

We don't need the Bible to tell us that. We have seen it with our own eyes. Humans are ingenious and resilient. We clear rocks from a field, build a wall, weed a garden, sweep a dirty street, rebuild a bridge, renew a dilapidated neighborhood, invent wind turbines and solar panels, organize a vaccination campaign, reconcile warring parties, mitigate mental illness, create literature, dance, music, and art. We bring order out of chaos over and over again.

Yes, humans do atrocious and malicious things to ourselves and others. But we also work to make repairs, create beauty, cultivate life, and reduce suffering in countless ways. There's a vicious cycle, but there's also a virtuous cycle.

Genesis 1 may be fiction or myth, but it nonetheless conveys a moral and spiritual truth. There is a way out of darkness and chaos.

*No one will save us, but we can save ourselves. We have divine-like powers. It takes work. It takes planning. It takes time.*

And that, I believe, is the gospel: suffering can be transformed by human hands, intelligence, ingenuity, and perseverance.

The Hebrew deportees did not give up or in. Many, not all, returned to Zion and rebuilt their city and their community.

That's an example of creative transformation from the past. Here's a more recent one.

In May 1980 a drunk driver killed Candace Lightner's thirteen-year-old daughter, Cari. Lightner was overwhelmed by grief and anger.

Not easily but somehow, Lightner managed a positive response to the unspeakable loss and suffering. She created Mothers Against Drunk Drivers, an organization dedicated to reducing the risk of such deaths. Other mothers joined. MADD advocates for tougher laws against drinking and driving and stricter enforcement of those laws. Following the creation of MADD the number of alcohol-related highway deaths in the Unites States has diminished dramatically.

Similar responses and organizations arose in the wake of the massacre of children at Sandy Hook Elementary school in 2012, the massacre of students at Marjory Stoneman Douglas High School in 2018, and the murder of George Floyd by a Minneapolis policeman in 2020.

None of that was easy. It took resilience, ingenuity, and hard work.

The parable of creation was placed at the beginning of the Old Testament because our Hebrew ancestors understood that life can be hard, sometimes very, very hard and harsh. The parable is good news for hard times. It doesn't pretend all is well because it isn't. The parable begins in darkness but doesn't end there.

*You are good. You are capable. You have creative powers. You have a dominion.*

🍎 🍎 🍎

So what about this "dominion" thing? Hasn't that precipitated a lot of problems for the earth and its creatures?

Yes, it has.

Dominion, however, is not what many people think it is. To "have dominion" is not a license to exploit and destroy.

Dominion is not domination.

When a monarch gives someone dominion over a portion of his kingdom, that agent is responsible and accountable to the monarch for the stewardship of the realm. The "Dominion of Virginia" in America was given to Lord Fairfax, but he was accountable to King George. Dominion is a responsibility to care for something belonging to another, not a license to abuse or exploit it. The parable of creation advocates responsibilities, not rights.

It's worth noting that in Genesis all the animals are declared good and blessed before the human animal arrives. Evolution and Genesis agree. Without the other animals leading the way, we wouldn't even be here. We owe them a deep debt of gratitude. We owe them our lives. They are companions and benefactors. We are responsible for their care and protection.

Dominion is not domination.

Tragically, many partisans of Christianity haven't understood this. They take dominion as a license to exploit. The earth is my food pantry and landfill, they think. I'm entitled. The Bible says so, they say. It doesn't. That misconstruing of "dominion" has led to policies and practices that have done great harm to the earth and its creatures.

Sacred texts matter. How we interpret them matters more.

There's yet one other traditional interpretation to reexamine before we exit this chapter.

Contrary to what many Christian theologians have claimed, God did not create *ex nihilo* (out of nothing), at least not according to Genesis 1. The literal translation of the Hebrew verb form (create) is "began creating." So it's not: "In *the* beginning God created" (at a single point in time). It should be: "When God *began creating*, the earth was a formless void. Darkness covered the waters." (Genesis 1.1) Creation began with existing stuff, dark material, as does our own creative work.

According to the Cambridge Dictionary, if we say we are in a dark place, it means we are unhappy or having difficult problems. For example, *I lost my job and my friends. I found myself in a very dark place. I looked for a light at the end of the tunnel.* Darkness can represent suffering.

Creation begins with darkness. "Darkness covered the deep." Still, God didn't eliminate darkness. God named it. And God called the darkness "night." (Genesis 1.5) And sometimes that's all we can do. We name the darkness and let it be. In time, light appears. Not overnight. But eventually. Day and night belong together. We can't have one without the other.

Judaism was not the first or only tradition to recognize this truth. Buddhism also acknowledges suffering as grist for creative, transformative work. Buddhism's first noble truth is: *Existence is suffering.* According to Judaism and Buddhism, suffering must be acknowledged and faced, not denied or avoided.

Friedrich Nietzsche (1844–1900) understood this as well. "Things must suffer, go dark, perish before they live again. This is not an escape or respite from life but rather its realization."

We can worry ourselves endlessly over the whys and wherefores of suffering. Many do and many have. Or we can work on transforming our suffering into something positive. Somehow.

As Dorothy Day, peace advocate and founder of the Catholic Worker Movement, put it: "No one has the right to sit down and feel hopeless. There's too much good work to be done."

Yes, indeed, there is much good work to be done. And it's all in keeping with the Jewish tenet *tikkun olam,* which means "repair the world." Or as Joan Chittister, the Benedictine monastic, put it: "We work because the world is unfinished and it is ours to develop."

Finally, to paraphrase a passage from the Holocaust survivor Victor Frankl's book *Man's Search for Meaning* (1946): *There is no meaning in suffering. But when we seek to transform suffering, we discover meaning.* Frankl himself transformed his traumatic suffering in a concentration camp into a book that has helped thousands of people find meaning in their lives.

The rebuilding of Jerusalem after the Babylonian Exile, Mothers Against Drunk Drivers, Black Lives Matter, and Frankl's book are a few of countless examples of turning suffering into something positive.

Genesis 1 is the gospel truth. The world is good. Humans are good.

But if humans are so good, why do we inflict harm on ourselves, others, and the world?

Are humans flawed somehow?

Yes.

And that's where we turn next.

🍎 🍎 🍎

CHAPTER 7

# Reframing Genesis 2–11

Genesis 1 depicts human capability. Genesis 2–11 depicts human vulnerability in five tales: Adam's rib, the forbidden fruit, the murder of Abel, the flood, and the tower of Babel. These stories temper the preceding paean to human nobility—not with pessimism but with realism. The stories are fictitious, but like the parable of creation they convey spiritual and psychological insights.

These tales were initially transmitted orally in various versions, beginning perhaps as early as the third millennium BCE. They likely developed independently of each other. But in the sixth century BCE (during the Babylonian Exile) these disparate tales were collated and transcribed in a final, official version and linked with each other in what would become chapters 2–11 in the book of Genesis. The tales are etiological—backstories explaining human nature. They were meant to be entertaining, engaging, and edifying.

*Why are humans different from other animals? Why do humans wear clothes? How did animals get their names? Why do men subjugate women? Why do people kill each other? Why do peoples and tribes mistrust each other? Why can't we all just get along?*

We may consider them fiction. But in antiquity people did not distinguish history from myth, logos from mythos, as we do. These stories simply made sense and rang true in their original cultural milieu. Supernaturalism was a given.

*Of course God created Eve out of Adam's rib. How else did the first woman get here? Of course the first humans disobeyed God and were punished. Of course animals can't sin and can't feel guilt; we can. Of course people are tempted to sin, animals aren't. Of course God gave us multiple languages to keep us apart.*

These tales are enigmatic. And most interpretations of them are benign, not harmful. But occasionally certain interpretations in the hands of powerful persons touting their views as THE WORD OF GOD have been harmful. For example, I've heard preachers say that because Adam was created before Eve, women are inferior, and subject to men. First is better than second!

In the following pages I debunk that and certain other harmful interpretations of these tales. Seeing Genesis 2–11 as a dramatic sequel to Genesis 1 reframed the whole narrative for me.

I first saw the linkage between chapter 1 and chapters 2–11 while attending Fuller Seminary in 1970. I read of it in Gerhard von Rad's book *Old Testament Theology* (1960). According to von Rad, the five tales in Genesis 2–11 present a diagnosis of the human condition. Each tale, he asserts, identifies a human problem: loneliness, guilt, anger, corruption, and tribalism. In each of the tales God intervenes with a gracious remedy to help the human creature carry on—in every tale, that is, except the final one, the tower of Babel.

Why is a remedy missing there? We'll look at that later.

Von Rad's explication of the tales is theistic: *Life is hard, but God is gracious. God will save us.* That's a theological analysis.

My interpretation is humanistic: *Life is hard, but humans are resourceful. Humans find ways to save themselves.* Humans create remedies.

As Thomas Hobbes (1588–1679) declared in *Leviathan* (1651), "Life is nasty, brutish and short." Consequently, as he also said, humans form societies to make life less nasty, brutish, and short. We create communities and institutions to ensure our survival and enhance our well-being.

It's what humans do and have done over the course of our existence.

Genesis 1–11 is like a two-act play.

Act 1: Human glory (Genesis 1)

Act 2: Human tragedy (Genesis 2–11)

🍎 🍎 🍎

CHAPTER 8

# Finding a Soulmate

## Act 2: Human tragedy; Scene 1: The Garden of Eden

*In the day that the Lord God made the earth and the heavens, when no plant of the field was yet in the earth and no vegetation of the field had yet sprung up—for the Lord God had not caused it to rain upon the earth, and there was no one to till the ground, but a stream would rise from the earth and water the whole face of the ground—then the Lord God formed man from the dust of the ground and breathed into his nostrils the breath of life, and the man became a living being. And the Lord God planted a garden in Eden, in the east, and there he put the man whom he had formed. Out of the ground the Lord God made to grow every tree that is pleasant to the sight and good for food, the tree of life also in the midst of the garden, and the tree of the knowledge of good and evil. . . . Then the Lord God said, "It is not good that the man should be alone; I will make him a helper as his partner."* (Genesis 2.4–9, 18. See appendix for full text.)

G enesis 2 is another creation story. And that's a problem for those who read the Bible literally because this one is different from the first one.

Which story is true?

Both.

One is about one thing; the other about something else. One depicts human capacity. The other depicts human fragility.

The two narratives differ in several significant ways.

First, in Genesis 1 God is personified as an emperor aloof from the world, calling things into existence with speech. "Let there be

65

light." "Let the waters under the sky be gathered in one place." And so on. In Genesis 2 God is personified as a potter, forming things with hands. "God formed man from the dust of the ground and breathed into his nostrils."

In Genesis 1 the Hebrew name of God is "Elohim." In Genesis 2 it's "Yahweh."

Second, in Genesis 1 man arrives at the end of the sixth day— *after* all the other animals. In Genesis 2 man arrives *before* all the other animals. Genesis 2 is not framed by a seven-day week. Genesis 1 is.

Third, Genesis 1 begins with chaos, darkness, and unruly waters. Genesis 2 begins with a paradisal garden of trees.

Fourth, in Genesis 1 God creates humankind—male and female— to exercise dominion over the whole of creation. "Let them have dominion." In Genesis 2 God needs someone to tend the garden of fruit-bearing trees, a relatively small vocation compared with the universal dominion of Genesis 1. The first human creature is Adam—a solitary creature without gender and not paired with another as in Genesis 1, where male and female are created simultaneously.

By the way, many people assume the first creature in Genesis 2 is the "first man." But that's not the case. Not yet. "Adam" derives from the Hebrew, *adamah,* meaning "soil." Adam is an "earthling," neither male nor female—even though *adamah* is masculine. (All Hebrew nouns are gendered.) The Hebrew nouns for "man" (*ish*) and "woman" (*isha*) don't appear until later in the story.

Finally, in Genesis 1 the divine voice proclaims again and again that everything is "good." "Behold it is good." "Behold it is good." In Genesis 2 the Potter says: "This isn't good." That alone—the juxtaposition of good and not good—should get our attention.

What isn't good in the idyllic Garden of Eden?

Loneliness.

"It isn't good for the earthling to be alone," the Potter laments.

The earthling has everything a body could want. It is *paradise*, after all. But, alas, something is missing. As it turns out, humans can't live on bread alone or even endless bread or anything else alone. Material prosperity and satiation will not satisfy humans. Our needs are more than physical.

Adam had everything but lacked a companion.

Aloneness is one thing, loneliness something else. Most of us need and desire friends, companions, society. Yes, we enjoy solitude. But we enjoy companionship too. Companionship is a basic human need.

Adam had no companion.

And that's "not good."

So the Potter fashions one animal after the other, hoping to remedy the earthling's problem. Each animal is paraded before the human for appraisal. I don't know whether this tale was meant to be humorous, but I think it could be told that way.

Adam, look what I made for you. Can this be your friend and companion?

*I don't know. Let me look.*

Well?

*No.*

What about this one?

*No.*

This one?

*No.*

In the process, as the text says, "Man gave names to all the animals."

What about this one?

Adam hesitates. Stares. Contemplates.

*I do like this one. This one shall be called "dog."* (Long pause.) I'm thinking this may be the one. (Another long pause.) *On second thought, no. It won't do as a soulmate. Sorry.*

None of the candidates suits. A helpmate for Adam is not found among the animals.

Despite the Potter's best efforts, the earthling is still alone.

This is serious, says the Potter to no one in particular. The earthling desperately needs a helper, a partner, a companion. I must try something else.

So the Potter puts the earthling to sleep and removes a rib. The Potter is now a plastic surgeon, a sculptor of a different kind. From Adam's rib the Potter sculpts a woman.

Adam awakes.

At that moment the earthling recognizes sexual differentiation. *This is bone of my bone, and flesh of my flesh. This one shall be called "woman"* (*isha,* in Hebrew).

The expression "bone of my bone, flesh of my flesh" is rare in the Bible. The only other uses are for blood relatives. This "other" is different but also alike. Akin. There is no mention of sexual reproduction. No order to procreate and fill the earth as there was in Genesis 1. Love and affection are the emphasis of this tale.

Adam and Eve were "helpmates" for each other. Soulmates.

Problem solved.

What does this story signify? Many answers are possible, but they are not all equally valid.

One summer during my college days I worked as a time clerk in a steel mill. An older coworker learned of my interest in the Bible and volunteered his opinion of the Adam and Eve story. In his opinion the word "Adam" really meant "atom." "That's what God created first, the atom," he told me proudly. "It's right there in the Bible! Atom and Adam have the same root meaning."

(No, they don't!)

He was entitled to his opinion. And I was entitled to disregard it as nonsense. I didn't tell him so. I simply said, "Interesting. I hadn't thought of that before."

Most of Christendom has seen this story as the "natural" basis for heterosexual marriage. "Therefore a man shall leave his parents and cling to his wife." (Genesis 2.24). *It's Adam and Eve, they say, not Adam and Steve! Same-sex marriage is forbidden—it's sinful according to this text.*

I disagree. This text is not about marriage at all. The story depicts the primal human need for companionship, not for marriage. The story is about love, not sex. Procreation is not mentioned. In fact, children do not appear until two scenes later.

If marriage is desired to secure or sanctify a companionship, so be it. But that's a social arrangement, not a natural one. Breeding is natural. Companionship is natural. Marriage is not.

Marriage is a social construct, one of many human inventions to preserve and protect life—to make it less "nasty, brutish and short." And, it must be said, divorce was invented for the same reason. As Voltaire (1694–1778) said: "Divorce is probably of nearly the same date as marriage. I believe, however, that marriage is some weeks the more ancient."

We all need companions. We don't all need spouses.

As Stephen Greenblatt put it in *The Rise and Fall of Adam and Eve* (2017): *There is nothing complicated or obscure here; everyone should be able to grasp its meaning. "Loneliness is the first thing which God named not good." The principal end of marriage is neither sex nor children; it is companionship. A solitary Adam, though he dwelt in Paradise, would have been condemned to unhappiness. It was, as Milton put it, for the "prevention of loneliness to the mind and spirit" that God created woman and brought her as a helpmeet to the man.*

In this story both genders emerge simultaneously—there is no "man" (*ish*) until there is "woman" (*isha*). Furthermore, as if to emphasize the equality of each gender (which may or may not have been intended), the woman emerges from a rib, not a foot bone or a head bone. Ribs are near the heart. Eve and Adam are meant to stand side by side, heart to heart—neither dominant or subordinate.

In most of the world, however, patriarchy prevails. The subjugation of women may be conventional and traditional, but according to this tale, it is not natural. Equality is.

Sadly, many traditional wedding vows—derived in part from this folktale—still require a woman to pledge submission to her husband just because he is "the first sex" and thus superior to "the second sex." In many traditional vows the groom promises to honor the bride while the bride promises to honor *and obey* the groom as mandated in the New Testament book of Ephesians (5.22–24). Where some see equality in this ancient tale, others, unfortunately, see hierarchy and thus a rationale or prescription for patriarchy sanctioned by THE WORD OF GOD.

Notably the implicit equality in this tale echoes the parable of creation, which explicitly affirms that both male and female are created in God's image. (Genesis 1.27) Both are like God, not just the male. Both, not just the male, are given dominion. In Genesis 1 male and female are equally endowed with dignity, divine-like status. In other words, according to the first two chapters of the Bible, one gender is not superior to the other.

(Boy, did a lot of people get that wrong!)

Of course, we don't need the Bible to validate what we already know to be right. But it does help when a venerable voice is on the right side of things. We wouldn't mind having Plato and Aristotle on our side as well. But on the subject of gender equality, they are on the wrong side. They definitely considered women inferior to men. No ambiguity from them.

Inferior.

Period.

Ecclesiastical officials ignored Bible-based equality, and by cherry-picking other biblical passages, they declared men superior to women. The Bible was used to sanction oppression of women.

But then patriarchy, as well as war and slavery, existed long before the arrival of the Bible. We can't blame war, patriarchy, and the oppression of women solely on the Bible. In fact, the Bible has been cited here and there, now and then, to support the liberation of women and enslaved people and to oppose wars. Sadly, those are exceptions.

This scene concludes with Adam and Eve "naked and unashamed," unselfconscious like the other animals. That would change, thanks to Eve.

🍎 🍎 🍎

# CHAPTER 9

# Eve Is a Hero

## Act 2: Human tragedy; Scene 2: The forbidden fruit

*Now the serpent was more crafty than any other wild animal that the Lord God had made. He said to the woman, "Did God say, You shall not eat from any tree in the garden?" The woman said, "We may eat of the fruit of the trees in the garden, but God said, You shall not eat of the fruit of the tree that is in the middle of the garden, nor shall you touch it, or you shall die." But the serpent said to the woman, "You will not die, for God knows that when you eat of it your eyes will be opened, and you will be like God, knowing good and evil."*

*So when the woman saw that the tree was good for food and that it was a delight to the eyes and that the tree was to be desired to make one wise, she took of its fruit and ate, and she also gave some to her husband, who was with her, and he ate. Then the eyes of both were opened, and they knew that they were naked, and they sewed fig leaves together and made loincloths for themselves.* (Genesis 3.1–7. See appendix for full text.)

🍎 🍎 🍎

When we left the last scene, Adam and Eve were naked and unashamed, like any other animal. But unlike other animals, in this scene they have a moral imperative hanging over their heads: *"You may eat of any tree in the garden, but you must not eat from the tree of knowledge or you will die."* (Genesis 2.15–16)

Animals know it's safe to eat some things but not other things. It's a matter of health, not morality. As far as we know, only the human animal has a conscience and thus is susceptible to guilt. Most of us fear the consequences of violating our own or society's moral code. Other animals know fear but they do not fear

73

retribution or feel remorse for violating a moral code (as far as we can tell).

In nature there is no "ought"; there is only "is." Stabbing *is* hurtful. Yes, it is. *Therefore we ought not to stab others.* The "therefore" is not in nature. It's in our minds. We create the "therefore." Good and evil, right and wrong are human constructs. But not in this story. In this story God determines what is right and wrong.

The prohibition is clear, and yet Eve consciously disobeyed the divine command. She took the forbidden fruit. Who can blame her? We all know that the forbidden is always the most alluring.

Did God not know this?

(I was forbidden to date Catholic girls in high school. Naturally, they were the most alluring.)

Eve stared at the tree. She dithered. And then a silver-tongued serpent standing on its hind legs urged her to pluck a fruit. (What a fun story!)

*I know God said you'd die if you ate that fruit. But I've been around here a long, long time. I've seen and heard things. And I'm telling you: You won't die. The truth is: You will be like God.* (Genesis 3.4, paraphrased)

Ah, yes, there it is—our moral quandary highlighted in one telling scene beneath a tree. What is right and what is wrong? Who knows best what we should do? Whose voice do we heed? Our own or another's? Whom can we trust?

Eve trusted the serpent. She made a choice. She defied God and, by extension, anyone else who would ever tell her what she could and could not do. She took the forbidden fruit and offered it to Adam. They both ate and "their eyes were opened." They saw themselves and the world as never before. It made them human.

They were suddenly self-aware and scurried for cover. They hid. Apparently, they knew something they hadn't known before, and it frightened them.

In the evening God came strolling through the garden. *Adam, where are you?* (Did God not know?) Their Maker found them. *Why are you hiding from me? Have you eaten from the forbidden tree?*

Yes, I have, Adam replied. But I only ate it because that damn woman gave it to me.

Yes, I did, Eve retorted. But I only took it because that damn serpent tricked me.

The serpent said nothing. It crawled away on its belly, never to walk erect again.

Many see this tale as a tragedy. It's known in Christian tradition as "the Fall," which presumes the first two humans (Adam and Eve) were once, however briefly, in mint condition—pristine, flawless, incorruptible, unspoiled, sinless—and then by sinning against God (eating the forbidden fruit) they fell from innocence into guilt, from grace into disgrace. That's a myth, of course, and yet universally true. After all, we all stumble and fall in one way or another from our "better self." We disgrace ourselves. We are ashamed. Often. But we can get back on our feet, again and again. No, we can't be "perfect," but we can be good.

Sin is a misstep. It is not fatal. We can brush ourselves off and get back on the right path again. At least that's the way Judaism tends to see it.

Tragically, the church fathers didn't see it that way. They considered humankind permanently damaged and vile. They summarized humankind's condition in a memorable couplet included in school primers: "In Adam's fall, we sinned all." It says "Adam," but the church meant "Eve."

*I do not permit a woman to teach or to have authority over a man; she is to keep silent. For Adam was formed first, then Eve, and Adam was not deceived, but the woman was deceived and became a transgressor.* (1 Timothy 2.12–14)

Many Christian children were weaned on this. I was.

Alas, Eve, not Adam, was designated the culprit in humankind's corruption. Church fathers declared that every single human is doomed from birth because of Eve, the first woman, the first mother, and the first sinner. According to orthodox Christianity, Eve was a bad apple who contaminated everyone else with "original sin."

Eve as the first villain.

But the story doesn't have to be read that way.

I see Eve as a hero. According to this mythic story, because of her, humanity no longer lives in darkness, no longer stumbles along blindly. Eve opened our eyes.

And that's no small matter.

"Sight" is the supreme metaphor for knowledge. *Oh, now I see!* And "insight" is the metaphor for self-understanding, the aspiration of nearly every religion and spiritual practice. As the former English slaveholder John Newton (1725–1805) put it in "Amazing Grace": *I once was blind but now I see!*

Eve gave us sight. Eve opened the door to insatiable curiosity. If we value humanity's persistent quest for knowledge, information, and insight, Eve is a hero.

Of course, this "event" is set in the fictional world of the Garden of Eden. In the real world there never was a single person or single event that sparked humankind's thirst for knowledge. Our inquisitive minds developed through the evolution of the brain. Neurology, however, is exposition. The Garden of Eden is poetry.

The authors of the forbidden tree tale might not have seen Eve as a hero. But I do. And so did the twentieth-century Jewish psychologist Eric Fromm. In *You Shall Be as Gods* (1966) Fromm frames this tale as humanity's *rise*, not its fall—an ascent, not a descent. For him it depicts a positive, distinctive trait of humankind, namely, persistently reaching for knowledge—a noble, not an ignoble, characteristic of humanity. And Eve is its champion.

But, alas, powerful Christian men (such as Saint Augustine, Bishop of Hippo) said Eve was guilty of *the* original sin. Women were demonized, scapegoated, and constrained in many "Christian" societies.

The subjugation of women (or anyone) is evil. As I mentioned earlier, such abuse existed long before the Bible arrived on the scene. We can't blame patriarchy solely on the Bible. But the Bible lent it sanctimony.

For millennia Christian theologians and preachers declared that because of Eve's sin, every child born thereafter was contaminated and condemned to eternal damnation. Original sin. Doomed— unless the cure was administered in time.

And what would that cure be?

The Sacrament of baptism.

And who could administer it?

Only the authorized (male!) agents of the Church.

And that, as it turns out, is one of the greatest scams of all time.

And it persists to this day.

The Catholics and the Orthodox have their baptismal cure. Evangelicals have their "sinner's prayer" cure. In either case you're doomed if you don't take the cure.

The Church might condemn Eve. God did not.

In this Garden tale, God did not sentence Adam and Eve to hell, death, or damnation. The Maker had sympathy for them.

God noticed the fig leaves they'd sewn to make loincloths. Which means, Adam and Eve had figured out how to "cover their shame" without any help from God.

The first cover-up.

Alas, humans not only cover skin with clothing; we shroud ourselves with personas. We pretend to be something we're not. We project images of ourselves. And that's not necessarily bad. The naked truth is not always bearable. We have a propensity to dress up our real self.

For better or worse, humans are imaginative and resourceful.

Adam and Eve sewed fig leaves.

But fig leaves are ephemeral. They don't last long. So God made them coverings from animal skins to better protect them as they wandered in exile, in an untamed world. East of Eden. They were vulnerable. They needed protection. They were learning how to survive in a nasty and brutish world. And they would keep on learning, making, and mending.

See how gracious God is, say the theists.

See how resourceful humans are, say the humanists.

Adam and Eve left the garden. Death was before them. The tree of life was behind them. God placed cherubim with flaming swords to guard the way to the tree of life.

Guard against what?

Scene 2 ends. No one died. That would change.

# CHAPTER 10

# The Birth of Violence

**Act 2: Human tragedy; Scene 3: Cain kills Abel**

*Now the man knew his wife Eve, and she conceived and bore Cain, saying, "I have produced a man with the help of the Lord." Next she bore his brother Abel. Now Abel was a keeper of sheep, and Cain a tiller of the ground. In the course of time Cain brought to the Lord an offering of the fruit of the ground, and Abel for his part brought of the firstlings of his flock, their fat portions. And the Lord had regard for Abel and his offering, but for Cain and his offering he had no regard. So Cain was very angry, and his countenance fell. The Lord said to Cain, "Why are you angry, and why has your countenance fallen? If you do well, will you not be accepted? And if you do not do well, sin is lurking at the door; its desire is for you, but you must master it."* (Genesis 4.1–7. See appendix for full text.)

🍎 🍎 🍎

The first parents took a forbidden fruit. The first child took a life.

Cain killed his brother, Abel, in cold blood because he Cain had been treated unjustly. Cain was angry and resorted to violence to right the wrong.

(Again, this is psychology, not history.)

Violent behavior is a primal human propensity. It's a bloody thread running through history and running through the Bible. It begins in Genesis with Cain's murder and continues through Revelation, the last book in the Bible—the bloodiest, most violence-riddled book in the Bible. It may be metaphorical, but it's still gruesome.

What prompts violence?

The story of Cain and Abel suggests an answer.

Once upon a time, Cain presented fruit to the Lord. Abel presented an animal. Abel was a herder. Cain a farmer. Each presented something they had nurtured, something of value. Abel's offering was accepted. Cain's was rejected.

The tale doesn't say why one offering was acceptable and the other not. It includes nothing like: *Bring meat, preferably a lamb! Do not bring fruit or vegetables!*

The judgment seems arbitrary, as many judgments are—or are *felt* to be. And that may be the author's intent. Life isn't fair. It just isn't. The focus of this tale is on Cain's reaction and his response to perceived injustice.

*Cain was very angry, and his countenance fell.*

Cain represents all who feel mistreated in this world and consequently harbor anger and resentment. Most people don't get angry without provocation. Injustice triggers anger. And anger triggers violence.

*Cain was very angry. He rose up and killed his brother.*

Anger is a healthy and natural reaction to injustice. When we or those we love are treated unjustly, we react with anger. Or should. Pity the one who feels no anger over injustice.

Anger is not a sin. It's a virtue, not a vice. Wrath, on the other hand, is designated as sin, one of the seven deadlies. Wrath is several degrees beyond anger. Wrath is anger marinated, churned, coddled. It's a volcano ready to erupt. Can anger be converted into something constructive? Or, as Jewish tradition asks: Can evil inclinations be tamed?

The Russian novelist and Nobel Prize-winner Alexander Solzhenitsyn (1918–2008) thought so. "There are plenty of reasons to hate the world, to blame somebody or something and seek revenge. But it's possible to transform anger into constructive action."

Reactions are one thing. Responses are something else. Reactions can't be helped. Responses can.

Can Cain master sin "crouching at his door" ready to devour him? Or will sin master Cain? Can Cain tame the beast that lurks in all of us?

The Cain and Abel story inspired John Steinbeck's *East of Eden* (1955). In that novel, one son, Aron, is beloved by his father and mother. The other son, Cal, is not. (Aron and Cal represent Abel and Cain, respectively.) The parents' favoritism seems arbitrary. It drives Cal to fits of despair. He wrestles with violent emotions.

Can Cal master the beast crouching at his door?

Cal is befriended by Lee, a Chinese man and longtime servant of Adam, the boys's father. One day Lee happens on the story of Cain and Abel in the family Bible. He is baffled by the pivotal Hebrew word *timshel*, translated "must." *Sin is lurking at the door; its desire is for you, but you MUST master it.* (Genesis 4.6–7, emphasis added.)

Lee wasn't convinced that "must" was apt. It was, after all, an English translation of a Hebrew word. And Lee knew that things are often misconstrued or lost in translation.

So Lee devoted himself to learning Hebrew. He also conferred with the elders of his Chinese community to tease out the most significant meaning of timshel, which is, like so many Hebrew words, multivalent. Lee discovered that *timshel* could mean "must," "shall," "can," or "may."

After reflecting on his own experiences, and after consulting with the elders, Lee settled on "may" as the most suitable translation. If *timshel* means "may," thinks Lee, the outcome of Cain's conflict is not inevitable. A choice is required.

Cal had a choice to make: succumb to or overcome the urge for revenge.

*Timshel.*

"You may."

Aron dies in World War I before Cal finds any resolution to his murderous feelings toward Aron. As the book reaches its final pages, Lee beseeches Adam to offer a blessing to his forlorn son. Adam dithers. And, then, just in the nick of time, he offers a blessing to Cal.

The last word in *East of Eden* is uttered by Adam on his deathbed. Adam whispers to his son:

*Timshel.*

You may.

🍎 🍎 🍎

The tale of Cain and Abel and the story of Cal and Aron suggest that few people explode without provocation. Injustice provokes anger.

Consider what happened in the United States on September 11, 2001.

The twin towers in New York City would not have been struck without provocation. But the dominant public question about the perpetrators of the attack was: *Why do they hate us so?*

In a *London Review of Books* article, a group of contributors each gave their views on the terrorist attacks. The historian Mary Beard argued that one should try to understand the terrorists's ideology. It served little purpose to decry the strikes as cowardly, she wrote, or just to write off the perpetrators as malevolent terrorists: "There are very few people on the planet who devise carnage for the sheer hell of it. They do what they do for a cause." The assaults should be comprehended not merely as an atrocity, she wrote, but as a response to Western foreign policy. (See *Making History: The Storytellers Who Shaped the Past,* by Richard Cohen.)

Anger is a primary propellant. Hatred is a byproduct.

Instead of asking, Why do they hate us, we might have asked, Why are they angry? Why do they resent us so? What have we done to provoke them?

(Such questions are not appropriate in all circumstances of violence—for example, child abuse, rape, or during a holocaust. But they are appropriate questions in the context of 9/11.)

Pursuing such questions would have shown us that U.S. policies and practices had not been as benign in the Middle East as the government had led its citizens to believe. Nefarious deals were made.

For example, the United States government supported the Shah of Iran (Mohammad Reza Pahlavi), a tyrant, for decades. In 1953 the CIA along with the United Kingdom's MI6 deposed Mohammad Mosaddegh, a pro-democracy leader elected as prime minister by the Iranian parliament. Furthermore, American and British companies extracted oil at great profit for themselves and far less for Iranians.

There's more.

Following the 1991 Gulf War, the United States government left five hundred and fifty thousand coalition troops stationed in Saudi Arabia—far more than the token troops stationed there for training missions since 1950. Osama bin Laden and other fundamentalist Muslims deemed the Western boots on the ground a desecration of their holy Muslim land, particularly Mecca and Medina. Muslims were angry. They felt mistreated by the imperialistic West. Anger simmered.

On September 11, 2001, resentments exploded.

The United States in turn was enraged. What would it do? It's hard to stop at "an eye for an eye." Unlimited retaliation is our default.

We might have asked: *What have we done to harm you? How can we make appropriate amends? And then we will tell you how you've hurt us?*

Of course, such an approach presumes a high level of maturity and spirituality. It's easier (and more instinctive) to retaliate. But it's not the only choice.

You many choose one way, or you may choose another.

*Timshel.*

Cain was angry. Cain brooded. Cain killed Abel.

That's understandable but not excusable.

God punished Cain, but he did not execute him. God assigned Cain to hard labor.

*"What have you done? Your brother's blood is crying out to me from the ground! And now you are cursed from the ground. When you till the ground, it will no longer yield to you its strength; you will be a fugitive and a wanderer on the earth."*

*Then Cain said to the Lord, "My punishment is greater than I can bear! Today you have driven me away from the soil, and I shall be hidden from your face; I shall be a fugitive and a wanderer on the earth, and anyone who meets me may kill me."* (Genesis 4.10–14)

In God's scheme, Cain would never settle down and feel at home anywhere, anyhow, any time.

But when God left, Cain said: *To hell with that.* He would not scratch a living from the soil or wander the earth like a fugitive. He would not be crippled by the curse. He defied the Lord just as his mother had.

*Cain built a city and named it Enoch after his son.* (Genesis 4.17)

Cain turned God's curse into a blessing. Was Cain a protohumanist?

From that "fictional" city arts, crafts, music, and science of sorts emerged. In a word, civilization. And that, as Hobbes suggested, is how humans make life less nasty, brutish, and short. But, alas, the city harbors a notorious murderer.

Civilization might mitigate our violent tendencies, but it can't eliminate them. Cain killed one person. Lamech, Cain's kinsman, killed a lot more, at least seven and possibly seventy times seven. (Genesis 4.14)

Violence procreates.

One of Lamech's sons, Tubal-Cain, a resident of Enoch, is known in tradition as forging the first sword. Armaments became an industry.

And that leads us to the next story.

# CHAPTER 11

# Violence Procreates

**Act 2: Human tragedy; Scene 4: The flood**

*The Lord saw that the wickedness of humans was great in the earth
and that every inclination of the thoughts of their hearts was only
evil continually. And the Lord was sorry that he had made humans
on the earth, and it grieved him to his heart. So the Lord said, "I will
blot out from the earth the humans I have created—people together
with animals and creeping things and birds of the air—for I am sorry
that I have made them." But Noah found favor in the sight of the Lord.*
(Genesis 6.5–8. The story of the flood occupies four chapters. The
verbiage itself is a deluge. See appendix for full text of Genesis 6–9.)

🍎 🍎 🍎

God was enraged by the violence that humans committed
constantly and rued the day he created them. God vowed
vengeance. God would destroy the world to save it.

Of course, violence had plagued the earth long before humans
arrived. Animals violently kill other animals for food and fight
viciously to protect their young.

God wasn't disgusted with the unpremeditated violence of other
animals. But, unfortunately, they would be collateral damage as so
many innocents are when "good guys" rain destruction down on
the "bad guys." In God's eyes, humankind alone was "corrupt" and
disgusting. Something in its nature had gone awry. We might say
evolution formed an unruly (and wicked) species.

God was angry. Sin was crouching at God's door. Would God
succumb to violence as Cain had?

*Timshel.*

Alas, God succumbed. God fell victim to the common delusion that violence can eliminate violence. We know exactly how God felt because many of us feel disgusted with humanity, especially with the vile and wicked people over there or in the other party. We deplore them. If only we—the pure and righteous—could eliminate all the bad people, the world would be so much better, we say.

Hence the National Rifle Association's slogan: *We need a good guy with a gun to stop a bad guy with a gun.*

Wouldn't you like to be in the room with a vote when that "good guy" is chosen? And who would that be? I'm guessing a Christian white guy.

(Oh, wait. How many mass murders have been instigated by such guys?)

As we know, no guy is all good. Each of us harbors a Dr. Jekyll and a Mr. Hyde. We are flawed. And God is flawed, too. God committed genocide.

(Not a good look for theism.)

Did a catastrophic flood actually happen in antiquity? Yes. Many, in fact. But not this particular one. It's fiction. It was likely appropriated from the much older Mesopotamian epic of Gilgamesh.

Noah and the flood can be seen as a parable. Dark but illuminating. And it seems more about us than God because it's we who grow frustrated with the world. We lash out. We save some. We abandon others. We destroy. And then we re-create.

In Genesis 1, God creates life out of water. In Genesis 6, God destroys life with water. The world reverted to chaos. Water covered the earth. Again.

The juxtaposition is artful. Life from water. Death from water.

And then the waters retreated. A dove flew from the ark and returned with an olive branch. Foliage appeared. And finally humans and the other animals arrived on the land. Again.

Water. Land. Foliage. Animals. People.

The post-deluge world is a metaphor for the cycle of chaos and order in our large and small worlds. Now and then we find ourselves under water, drowning. It's hard to breathe. And then, somehow, our feet are on solid ground, and we're rebuilding our life. Our world is green. Again.

Noah stepped onto a clean stage. It was time for a fresh start. Time to repair and rebuild. But first gratitude had to be expressed to God. So Noah took a knife and killed several of his animal companions—a sacrificial offering to God.

(Wait, wait. We were rescued for this?! You're actually genuflecting to the one who tried to wipe us all out?! The one who committed genocide?! That's your religion?)

*Noah built an altar to the Lord and took of every clean animal and of every clean bird and offered burnt offerings on the altar. And when the Lord smelled the pleasing odor, the Lord said, "I will never again curse the ground because of humans, for the inclination of the human heart is evil from youth; nor will I ever again destroy every living creature as I have done.*

*As long as the earth endures,*
*seedtime and harvest, cold and heat,*
*summer and winter, day and night*
*shall not cease."*
(Genesis 9.20–22)

God repented. Never again.

(This tale is so much like us. How many times have we said "never again"? And, yet, it's ever and ever again. What, then, shall we do?)

God said in so many words: *Humans will always be who and what they are. I'll just have to live with that and make the best of it.*

God hung a rainbow in the heavens to declare a truce.

(A good look for theism.)

After the storm, the rainbow.

Let's take a deep breath and begin anew. There's a lot of good work to be done.

Noah planted a vineyard.

Noah got drunk.

*Noah, a man of the soil, was the first to plant a vineyard. He drank some of the wine and became drunk, and he lay uncovered in his tent.* (Genesis 9.20–21)

When Noah awoke from his drunken slumber and learned that he had been observed with his pants down (a major taboo in that culture) by his son Ham, he put a curse on Ham's son, Canaan.

*You will be a slave to other nations!*

(Was Noah really the best God could find? Was God sober when Noah was chosen?)

With that curse, Noah—"a man who walked with God"—planted the seeds of oppression. Tragically, sanctimonious American Christians would cite the curse of Canaan to rationalize the brutal enslavement of Africans in the United States of America.

What?!

Yes, that's right.

Nineteenth-century slaveholders were told—by preachers from their pulpits, "scientists" from their universities, and theologians from their ivory towers—that descendants of Noah's cursed grandson Canaan ("lowest of slaves shall he be") migrated to Africa. They pointed to maps to prove it. Thus, Africans were Canaan's descendants! (Of course! Isn't it obvious?!) And so, according to many white Christians the Atlantic slave trade fulfilled biblical prophecy. The brutal practice of slavery was rationalized by THE WORD OF GOD.

The entire American South perpetrated that fraud for nearly three hundred years.

(For a detailed discussion and repudiation of this repugnant biblical interpretation, see *The Curse of Ham: Race and Slavery in Early Judaism, Christianity, and Islam,* by David Goldenberg, 2003.)

The story of the flood brings the trajectory of violence in Genesis 2–9 to a dramatic finale. Yes, the story is mythical, but it's also prescient. Annihilation is now a real possibility—if not by nuclear holocaust, then by climate catastrophe, or germ warfare, or the decimation of bees or ants.

Are humans capable of building a better world?

Yes. But not easily. Like Noah, we build with crooked timber.

That's not pessimism. That's realism.

*Timshel.*

🍎 🍎 🍎

# CHAPTER 12

# Human Resolve

**Act 2: Human tragedy; Scene 5: The tower of Babel**

*Now the whole earth had one language and the same words. And as they migrated from the east, they came upon a plain in the land of Shinar and settled there. And they said to one another, "Come, let us make bricks and fire them thoroughly." And they had brick for stone and bitumen for mortar. Then they said, "Come, let us build ourselves a city and a tower with its top in the heavens, and let us make a name for ourselves; otherwise we shall be scattered abroad upon the face of the whole earth." The Lord came down to see the city and the tower, which mortals had built. And the Lord said, "Look, they are one people, and they have all one language, and this is only the beginning of what they will do; nothing that they propose to do will now be impossible for them. Come, let us go down and confuse their language there, so that they will not understand one another's speech." So the Lord scattered them abroad from there over the face of all the earth, and they left off building the city. Therefore it was called Babel, because there the Lord confused the language of all the earth, and from there the Lord scattered them abroad over the face of all the earth.* (Genesis 11.1–9)

🍎 🍎 🍎

Although traditional interpretations have seen the tower of Babel negatively, it can also be seen as a parable of hope. The tower of Babel suggests that humankind is capable of great things—if we work together.

Once upon a time, all humans spoke one language. (We are in folktale land, again). They set out to build something great on the plain of Shinar. They began constructing a tower that reached toward the heavens. (The image was likely appropriated from ancient Babylon where ziggurats stood tall.)

The tower rose higher and higher, and suddenly the gods took notice. They felt threatened. *Come, let us go down and confuse their language there, so that they will not understand one another's speech.*

Let us go down. Us.

The jealous gods (polytheism is in play here) shattered the unity and community of humans, scattering them to the four corners of the earth, into bickering, warring tribes.

What follows is one of the saddest verses in the Bible.

*They left off building the city.* (Genesis 11.5)

Which raises the question: Is the curse fatal? Are we condemned forever to xenophobia?

God cursed Cain to a life of wandering.

Cain built a city. Cain overcame the curse.

Can humans overcome the curse of alienation?

Yes, we can.

Many theologians and preachers see the tower of Babel as an example of hubris. The builders were trying "to make a name for themselves," they say. Therefore, the curse was deserved. (Similarly, Prometheus was cursed for stealing fire from Zeus.)

Many Christians say it's a sin to presume too much, to think too highly of ourselves, to reach toward the heavens. (I'm all for humility, but not self-debasement.) But how will we know what's possible and what's not unless we keep trying to do great things? As the *Whole Earth Catalog's* statement of purpose puts it: "We are as gods and might as well get good at it."

The tower of Babel depicts an admirable characteristic of our species: cooperation. Despite divine warnings and curses, we mustn't apologize for Eve's grasping the forbidden fruit, or for Cain building a city, or for Noah regenerating the earth, or for the cooperative human effort to build the tower of Babel.

Babel gives us hope. We can build and rebuild, again and again as we did in London, Dresden, Hiroshima, Hanoi, New York City, New Orleans, and other places too numerous to name. We can reforest scarred landscapes. We can repopulate endangered species.

We're resilient and ingenious.

And we are fearful and suspicious of others.

Two truths.

We don't need the Bible to tell us how tribalism fractures the human family. In one sense, yes, it's a curse. But it's not imposed by God or the gods. We bring it on ourselves. No one is born with hatred or fear of others. We learn to hate. We learn to mistrust. We can unlearn them.

Well, we may or may not.

Tribalism is the way evolution wired us. It has survival benefits. We feel most safe within our own group. That's instinctive. But instincts can be overcome. Yes, we are tribal, but we don't have to be xenophobic.

No other animal species has the ability to work as cooperatively over long spans of time and large expanses of space as humans. Humans created the World Wide Web to share information expansively. We rapidly developed COVID-19 vaccines through international cooperation. We've linked distant parts of the globe by rails, roads, airports, and seaports. Twenty-nine nations collectively contributed $10 billion to enable the creation of the James Webb Space telescope successfully launched on December 25, 2021.

We know how to cooperate. And communicate.

Scientists, artists, and musicians have created global communities and networks among themselves in which race, religion, and language are no longer the barriers they once were. Humans create art, music, prosthetics, safe cars, safe planes, disease-resistant crops, fire-resistant houses, irrigation networks, levees, telegraphs, steam engines, solar panels, international trade agreements, and laws to protect the vulnerable from the ruthless. We've created organizations and institutions to cultivate community among traditionally antagonistic religions.

There are reasons for optimism.

But alas, all inventions are not positive. After all, it also takes cooperation and ingenuity to create an assault weapon, a bomb, poisonous gas, or germ warfare. We have the power to create *and destroy*. We launch wars of enormous death and destruction.

In our lifetime, the military-industrial-academia complex has become a golden goose. The war machine brings huge profits to a certain few. "War is good for business."

(Alas, greed may be even more pernicious than violent aggression.)

There are reasons for pessimism.

Yes, other animals kill and even "murder." Jane Goodall and other primatologists observed chimpanzees, mainly males, undertaking murderous rampages against fellow chimpanzees. But unlike humans, she says, chimpanzees do not plot violence *months in advance*. Chimpanzee aggression is reactive and adaptive. Human aggression is reactive, too, but also proactive.

What can be done?

Biological evolution works too slowly to eliminate our propensity for revenge any time soon. Cultural evolution, however, moves less slowly, even quickly sometimes. It outpaces biology. We can work on improving our cultures.

We have a great capacity for learning, adjusting, and adapting.

Education, training, medication, meditation, spirituality, and even religion can restrain or mitigate destructive behavior. Still, our instinct for vengeance hasn't changed in a hundred thousand years. So we must put cultural evolution into overdrive. The challenge is great.

But I'm hopeful.

I'm hopeful because as Goodall also noted: Every day millions and millions of humans plot good, working together to make the world more sustainable, more just, and more peaceful. And as far as I know, chimpanzees don't do that.

Humans plot good!

Indeed, many are working to restrain nuclear proliferation, to resolve conflicts, to rescue and assimilate refugees, to mitigate climate change. Many are working to make societies more equitable. Every day untold millions work for the good of all.

We can't eliminate tribalism, but we can confederate. In fact, we can celebrate and relish our diversity. We can build more bridges and fewer walls. Nature shows us how.

For more than 3.5 billion years the evolutionary process has been creating wider, more inclusive communities among earth's diverse creatures. As it turns out, cooperation is more prominent than competition in nature. The trajectory of nature is toward more inclusion, interconnectedness, and—as the Vietnamese Buddhist monk Thich Nhat Hanh (1926–2022) put it—"inter-being."

We can't "get back to the Garden." But we can get back to Babel. We can work together as one. Supernatural powers won't save us. Human ingenuity, resilience, and hard work might.

Religions and countries likely will never disappear, no matter how much we imagine it. Humanity will always speak multiple languages. So we might as well accept tribalism as a given, like gravity, and make the best of it.

Besides, who wants a world without diversity? Nature requires diversity to survive and thrive. A homogeneous world would diminish our joy and delight. Cultures, religions, languages, complexions, customs, tribes, peoples, and nations are part of the rainbow. Let's imagine tribes, peoples, nations, and religions confederating and cooperating. That's the path that leads to a better world.

That's hopeful realism.

Who will undertake that work?

And that leads us to an interlude before we take up the New Testament gospels.

🍎 🍎 🍎

# Interlude

Remember Gerhard von Rad's schematic interpretation of the five mythic tales in Genesis 2–11? Each tale had two parts, he noted. First, a human affliction is identified. Second, God provides a remedy—a companion is found for Adam; garments are provided to cover Adam and Eve's shame; a protective mark mitigates Cain's paranoia; and Noah's family is chosen to regenerate the earth after the apocalyptic flood.

Problem. Remedy.

But, alas, the tower of Babel fiasco ends without any remedy identified. Where is it? According to von Rad, the remedy is found in the opening verses of the next chapter. Remember: The Bible had no chapter breaks initially. They were added a thousand years later. So the tower of Babel tale flowed directly into this:

*Now the Lord said to Abram and Sarah, "Go from your country and your kindred and your father's house to the land that I will show you. I will make of you a great nation, and I will bless you, and make your name great, so that you will be a blessing. I will bless those who bless you, and the one who curses you I will curse; and in you all the families of the earth shall be blessed." (Genesis 12.1–3)*

And there's the remedy. All the families of the earth who live under the curse of Babel may yet be blessed. Which is to say, prosper and thrive.

Out of the blue (or from deep within) Sarah and Abraham heard a voice. Or was it a nudging, a hunch, or imagination?

Get going, said God.

And they went.

And with that we leave the world of timeless myths (Genesis 1–11) and enter the world of time and space—history in the making, even though that "history" will be constructed, refracted, and embellished.

At Genesis 12 we enter a story of a morally flawed people whose founders nonetheless undertook an experiment in building a world of peace, love, justice.

Who will save the broken human family?

A broken human family.

Humanists agree.

Some people count on God. Others count on humans. And some count on both.

Humanists believe humans, not God or the gods or any "outside force," will save the world. But what does it mean to be "saved?" Salvation in Judaism, unlike in Christianity, isn't about going to heaven instead of hell. It's mainly about making whole what is broken, including personal relationships, plus social, political, and ecological systems. It's about cultivating a world that is just, healthy, and wholesome.

(I once heard this summary of Judaism's worldview: *God was at the beginning. God will be at the end. Don't fret or fixate on either. Instead, work hard to make the in-between time as just, wholesome, and beautiful as you possibly can. Be here now. Fully.*)

The Jewish people were not the only ones to undertake a global humanitarian project. Many peoples, cultures, and religions had similar stirrings at about the same time. The philosopher Karl Jaspers (1883–1969) calls it the Axial Age. Versions of the Golden Rule appear nearly everywhere. Human consciousness was evolving. People were learning from experience. Knowledge and wisdom increased.

The Jewish people were devoted to both.

Genesis 1 depicts the creation of the world. Genesis 12 depicts the creation of Abraham and Sarah's family. They and their descendants believed they were chosen, not for status but for a function—to be a light to the world, to live and practice the Torah as revealed to Moses. That's one way to express chosenness, but it's not the only way.

As it turns out, nearly all tribes or peoples believe they are "the chosen" aornd "the real" people while other people are not. "Us versus them" is primal.

We're chosen. You're not.

Not so fast there.

Ponder this: Who isn't chosen to bless the world? According to Genesis 1, humanness includes chosenness as a covenantal obligation to creation and to our fellow creatures and the earth. It's our dominion, our responsibility. We are chosen to love and care for all, not because we're Jewish but because we're human. (Somehow a lot of us didn't get that memo. A lot of us missed that ennobling message in Genesis 1.)

To bless the world is your birthright. You are blessed. You are called. You are chosen. Now get over it and get on with the work of mending the world—the world-at-large and the world-at-small. Your world.

No, you are not the light of the whole world. No one is. But you are one particular light in a certain world of people, places, things, and problems—where you live and move and have your being. It's your vocation to care for *that* world with or without the Torah as your guide. As Mother Teresa said: "There are no great things to be done. But there are many small things to be done with great love."

Abraham and Sarah's family was flawed—corrupt, hypocritical, xenophobic, egotistical, and prone to violence. Hebrew scripture does not cover up their warts or wickedness. The Old Testament is honest, authentic, and often confessional.

The Israelites fought each other and fought their neighbors. They stood with each other and against each other. Some welcomed immigrants and strangers. Others brutally expelled indigenous people from their homes and land. Some advocated war. Some advocated peace. Some trampled orphans, widows, and the poor into the dust. Others lifted them up. Some expected a messiah to save them. Others did not.

Some remained theists. Some became atheists. Some became pantheists. Some became humanists.

In other words, they were like Americans—and every other nation on the face of the earth, with perhaps one exception: *The Jewish people had an extraordinary knack for telling, writing, and preserving their story.*

As the Old Testament shows, they tried to find a way to bless all nations without being arrogant or annoying. They failed. They were arrogant and annoying. Still, they planted and cultivated a powerful and noble idea:

*What does the Lord require of us but to do justice, love kindness, and walk humbly on this earth.* (Micah 6.8)

That seed is in all of us. Now and then it blossoms and bears fruit. Not everywhere at once. But here and there. Now and then.

And that brings us to the next section: Jesus and the gospels.

# CHAPTER 13

# First-Century Jewish Sects

Jesus was a child of Judaism. According to genealogies in Matthew and Luke, Jesus was a distant son of Abraham and Sarah. In the early part of the first century, his life, teachings, and work inspired the formation of a Jewish sect that eventually became the established Christian Church in the fourth century.

But initially it was just another sect competing with four older sects: the Zealots, the Sadducees, the Essenes, and the Pharisees. One question facing each sect was: How do we live and survive under the Roman occupation, under oppression and brutality? It was far from the only question, but it was an important one. Although many, maybe even most, Jews were unaffiliated with a sect, those four sects provided four distinct responses to "the Roman problem."

Fight. Collaborate. Flee. Differentiate.

Those responses are not unique to the first-century Jewish people. For example, they are similar to the responses of Muslims under the American occupation of Iraq in 2003, Indians under British rule in the early twentieth century, and enslaved Africans under the oppression of white slaveholders beginning in the seventeenth century in America.

Fight. Collaborate. Flee. Differentiate.

## Zealots

The Zealots engaged in armed rebellion against Rome—its officials and troops. They were inspired by Israel's legendary warrior chieftains such as Joshua, Gideon, and Samson, plus the warrior king David.

The Zealots were also inspired by the Maccabees. The Maccabees had undertaken an armed rebellion against the Greek-Syrian tyrant Antiochus Epiphanies in the second century BCE. They eventually routed the occupiers and then purged the temple in Jerusalem of its foreign desecration.

The Zealots were fighters. Carry a dagger. Kill Romans.

That's one response to oppression.

The Sadducees had a different response.

## Sadducees

The Sadducees collaborated with the Romans. *If you can't beat 'em, join 'em.* Many Sadducees became priests, guardians of the temple, and treasurers of its assets. They did well.

Like Muslims working in the "Green Zone" in Baghdad during the American occupation (2003–11), Sadducees worked in the "Roman Zone." They made deals. After all, the Sadducees valued the present more than the future, material rewards more than spiritual rewards. The Sadducees were materialists, not idealists, spiritualists, or supernaturalists. They did not believe in the afterlife.

The Sadducees revered only the five books of Moses and disregarded the rest of the Tanakh. Because they saw no reference to life after death in the books of Moses, they did not believe in it. Intimations of resurrection were in the "inferior" prophetic books such as Hosea and Ezekiel.

So, unlike most other Jews, the Sadducees did not believe in the resurrection of the dead. That may have driven them to accumulate rewards in this life. They got rich. They held power. And just as Iraqi collaborators were despised by many Muslims, so the Sadducees were despised by many Jews, especially the Zealots.

The Sadducees collaborated.

That's one response to occupation.

The Essenes had a different one.

## Essenes

The Essenes were escapists. They fled Judaea to seek a safe, uncontaminated life away from vile Romans and apostate Jews similar to how the Amish isolate themselves from the larger society lest the way of "the English" corrupt them and their children. The Essenes established a monastic-like community in Transjordan (east of the Jordan River).

They were admired by fellow Jews for their radical faithfulness and extreme adherence to Torah and the prophets. Some scholars believe that John the Baptist spent time with the Essenes, because like the Essenes, John urged Jews to come clean and start afresh on the path of righteousness through the ritual of full-body baptism in the Jordan River. Like the Essenes, John believed that the messiah was coming soon.

*His axe is in his hand! He will separate the wheat from the chaff!* (Matthew 3.10)

The Essenes yearned for deliverance by one or possibly two different messiahs—a warrior messiah like David and/or a priestly messiah like Aaron. At that time the notion of "messiah" wasn't sharply defined or confined to a single figure. Eventually, the Jesus sect would define it in shocking terms. No one thought messiah could win by losing. Whoever thought the messiah would let himself be crucified without a fight or a pledge of retribution?

The Essenes fled Roman occupation.

That's one response to occupation.

The Pharisees had a different one.

## Pharisees

The Pharisees determined to remain faithful to their tradition without taking up arms, without collaborating, and without forsaking society. If the Essenes were like the Amish in separating from society, the Pharisees were like the Mennonites— differentiating themselves through high moral standards within society. Pharisees (from the Aramaic *parushi* meaning "one who is separate") were highly respected by other Jews for their exceptional piety. In fact, the apostle Paul boasted about being a Pharisee.

*If anyone else has reason to be confident in the flesh, I have more: circumcised on the eighth day, a member of the people of Israel, of the tribe of Benjamin, a Hebrew born of Hebrews; as to the law, a Pharisee; as to zeal, a persecutor of the church; as to righteousness under the law, blameless.* (Philippians 3.4–6)

Pharisees venerated both the traditional scriptures (Law, Prophets, Writings) and an evolving oral tradition ("oral Torah")— elaborations of the written Torah. Jesus disparaged that oral tradition while creating his own, for example, in the Sermon on the Mount. ("You have heard it said, but I say unto you...") Nevertheless, in many respects Jesus was most akin to the Pharisees—although you'd hardly think so from the way the gospels portray them.

The Pharisees differentiated themselves *within* society by practicing exemplary piety. They were zealously faithful to the law and traditions.

Stay in place, practice piety, but keep your head down.

That's one response to occupation.

The Jesus sect had a different response

# CHAPTER 14

# The Jesus Sect

Like the Pharisees the members of the Jesus sect differentiated themselves within society. They stayed in place, but didn't keep their heads down. They boldly and loudly urged people to believe the kingdom of God was now, not later; that the Messiah was here, not somewhere else. Live in the present. Don't wait for the future.

The Jesus sect also taunted the Romans by proclaiming a kingdom and a king greater than their own. The Roman Empire is doomed. The end of its world is near as Jesus trumpeted in his "little apocalypse."

> *But in those days, after that suffering,*
> *the sun will be darkened,*
> *and the moon will not give its light,*
> *and the stars will be falling from heaven,*
> *and the powers in the heavens will be shaken.*

(Mark 13.24–25)

Like the Zealots, the Jesus sect organized in cells. Jesus sent his "troops" on missions, two by two, armed with the good news of the kingdom of God as superior to the kingdom of Rome. Like the Essenes, the Jesus sect advocated a righteousness "greater than the Pharisees." Like the Sadducees, it focused on the material world—food for the hungry, healing for the sick, and comfort for the distressed now—not pie in the sky by and by. And like the Pharisees, it did not forsake society. Furthermore, like the Pharisees, it honored the full spectrum of Hebrew scripture while disparaging the oral tradition propagated by them.

But that evolving body of oral tradition possibly prompted or inspired the novel sect to collect its own oral traditions to form the gospels. After all, the gospels, like the Pharisee's oral tradition, are extensions of the Tanakh.

Like other rabbis, Jesus started with the written Torah and stretched it. As he says in the Sermon on the Mount: *You have heard that it was said* [in Torah]*, but I say unto you*—a phrase he repeats several times. Yes, the written Torah says one thing, but I am telling you something else, something deeper in the law. *Don't murder, but also don't be angry. Don't commit adultery, but also don't lust. Love your neighbor, but also love your enemy.* (Matthew 5.21–48)

Jesus honored the Torah. Jesus was a respectful child of Judaism.

But he didn't hesitate to add his voice to the ongoing conversations. After all, in Judaism the more voices, the merrier. (In Christianity, not so much. The Church hunted down heretics. Judaism, not so much.) Jesus stood in an argumentative tradition. Interpretations abounded and rebounded.

*"Yes, I see what you're saying. But let me tell you what I think about that."*

*"Oh, I see what you're saying. So let me tell you what I think about that."*

And so on.

Today's conclusion is tomorrow's premise. Always.

Each of the five Jewish sects advanced an approach, an argument, a case, while competing for adherents. Consequently, the upstart Jesus sect was compelled to distinguish itself from the others, especially from the Pharisees, the more venerable sect, the sect most like itself. Thus, the novel sect turned minor disputes between itself (represented by the figure of Jesus) and the Pharisaic school into sharp antagonisms.

*Woe to you, scribes and Pharisees, hypocrites! For you tithe mint, dill, and cumin and have neglected the weightier matters of the law: justice and mercy and faith. It is these you ought to have practiced without neglecting the others. You blind guides! You strain out a gnat but swallow a camel!* (Matthew 23.23–24)

Small differences were exaggerated, rather like the exaggerated differences between competing church denominations or political parties.

*Baptists are too fervent! Episcopalians too tepid! The Democrats are socialists! The Republicans are fascists!*

In the gospels the Pharisees are portrayed as villains. Historically, however, the Pharisees were heroes among the Jewish people. In fact, they saved Judaism from extinction after the destruction of the temple by the Roman army in 70 CE. Out of the rubble, Pharisaic elders created rabbinic Judaism (which in various forms survives and thrives today). With no temple left, the Pharisees introduced household-based practices to keep their faith alive. Dispersed among various nations and people ("the Diaspora"), rabbinic Judaism provided a way for the Jewish people to differentiate themselves within diverse, and often hostile societies.

In the absence of Jesus, the novel sect did similar things. Partisans gathered in homes, told the stories of Jesus, recited his law of love, offered prayers, sang psalms, and partook of a sacramental meal (bread and wine). Those gatherings with their storytelling continued week and after week, year after year, in and beyond Judaea. And then finally, forty some years after Jesus's death, those oral stories found their way into the gospels.

And thus the novel sect produced promotional tracts (gospels) to win and influence people.

These Jewish sects argued in and among themselves and against each other. They were not, however, debating societies. They were more like American political parties (Democrat, Republican, Green) or movements (abolitionist, civil rights, environmental) than religious denominations (Baptist, Methodist, Catholic). A sect's concerns were for the welfare and survival of the nation, not so much for the reform of its religious life or rituals.

In fact, Jews at that time could not identify Judaism as a "religion." *I don't know what you mean by "religion." What's that?* They had a way of life, bolstered by rituals, codes, practices, and myths—but no "religion" per se.

If you asked almost any ancient peoples, for example Native Americans, what their "religion" was, you'd get a blank stare. "Religion" was the warp and weft of daily life. It was the sea they swam in. "Religion" as a distinct cultural category was not identified as such until the thirteenth century.

In the first century all Jewish people faced the same problems no matter their party or affiliation the way Americans face common problems no matter their party or religious affiliation. *How can we feed our families and keep them safe? How can we protect ourselves from enemies both foreign and domestic? How can I find relief from oppressive debt? What makes for a meaningful life?*

One existential question many Jews (especially in Judaea; not so much in Galilee) faced was: *How do we survive and live with dignity and integrity under the Roman occupation?* The Jesus sect, like the other four, claimed to know the best way to deal with the Roman occupation: Proclaim an alternative kingdom and live under its ruler and rules now. Live as though the kingdom is here and now.

*We are citizens of God's kingdom, not Rome's. Jesus is our king, not Caesar. Love is our ruler and our rule, not fear.*

And let us remember: Love is action, not just a feeling. We must love our enemies even though we hate them. And that takes training, as Gandhi and Martin Luther King Jr. understood so well. Jesus embodied and modeled the way of nonviolent resistance. It wasn't for everybody. It's a hard path to take.

Turn the other cheek? Go the extra mile? Not easy.

By the way, turning the other cheek to a so-called superior's back-handed slap and going the extra mile when compelled by a Roman soldier were actually acts of resistance, not submission. The "victim" assumes agency by startling and embarrassing the oppressor.

*I am a person! I will not grovel. I will hold my head high. I am who I am.*

The Zealots had one way to deal with the Romans. The Jesus sect had another.

To read the New Testament without the Roman occupation in mind is like reading the Declaration of Independence or Thomas Paine's *Common Sense* without the British domination of the American colonies in mind. In first-century Judaea, the Roman occupation was a serious issue. And because all people live under one kind of oppression or another, its story and message is timeless.

It's about loving others to death.

(Well, that may be an overstatement. Some in the Jesus sect hoped and prayed that God would obliterate their hated enemies. In other words, the sect was composed of human beings like us. They had mixed feelings and wobbly convictions. Not all were ready to walk the "way of the cross.")

Still, Jesus invited many to walk that way ("take up your cross and follow me") while never condemning anyone who couldn't. It was an invitation, not a mandate. Follow if you can. Don't watch me. Don't worship me. Come along with me. Don't believe *in me*. Believe *with me*. And if you can't join me (or the movement) now, maybe later.

# CHAPTER 15

# Is Jesus Historical or Fictional?

Initially, the gospels introduced Jesus to people living in the eastern Mediterranean world. Not surprisingly, the gospels mimic the mythologized stories of heroes of that world. Some of those heroes were divinized.

For example, temples were built to venerate Romulus, Julius Caesar, and Augustus. Furthermore, the parentage of such heroes was fabricated, mythologized. Gods impregnated mortal women who gave birth to immortal men. Thus, their offspring were called "son of god." And then following their deaths, these immortals were deified by public acclamation as they ascended to Olympus, the abode of the gods.

The story of Jesus hews to that trajectory.

Romulus, Julius, and Augustus were enshrined in part to encourage emulation of their virtues—bravery in battle plus charity, justice and compassion for the masses. Similarly, members of the novel sect divinized Jesus in part to encourage emulation of his virtues—nonviolence ("forgive them for they know not what they do"), compassion for the suffering ("and he touched the leper"), acceptance of all people ("let the little children come unto me and do not hinder them!"). In their hands, Jesus became larger than life.

In his day, however, Jesus was not widely known. Next to nothing is recorded about him outside the New Testament. Ultimately, the gospel writers made him into a global phenomenon.

The Roman Jewish historian Josephus (37–100 CE) makes a passing reference to Jesus's brother James and to Pontius Pilate in his *Jewish Antiquities* (ca. 94). The Roman senator Tacitus refers to people who are called Christians by the populace in his *Annals* (ca. 116 CE). He refers to Jesus as "Christus, from whom the name

[Christian] had its origin, [and who] suffered the extreme penalty during the reign of Tiberius at the hands of one of our procurators, Pontius Pilatus." (Book 15, chapter 44)

Jesus would have been lost to history except for the creative rhetorical and literary efforts of his "school." It wouldn't let him die, just as the schools of Socrates, Plato, and Aristotle wouldn't let their respective teachers die, which is to say, be forgotten. In the gospels Jesus comes to life.

Keep in mind: Jesus was first and foremost a child of Judaism. He amplified parts of his inherited tradition while ignoring other parts—a good model for any recipient of any type of tradition. Jesus and the new sect amplified and advanced certain venerable Jewish ideals embedded in its people's lore and scriptures, including love, justice, and mercy.

(By the way, the popular notion that the Old Testament is about a God of wrath while the New Testament is about a God of love is not only simplistic, it's wrong. The Old Testament often portrays God as merciful, long-suffering, broken-hearted, eager to gather the vulnerable under her wings like a mother hen.)

(Furthermore, the Old Testament knows of no fiery hell where sinners are tormented endlessly. The New Testament does. Of course, Jesus is about love, but he also condemns certain people to a fiery hell "where the worm never dies, and the fire is never quenched." There's nothing in the Old Testament like the graphic depiction of hell in the New Testament book of Revelation. Much more could be said on this matter, but I simply want to correct a long-standing, anti-Semitic prejudice against the Old Testament. Yes, the Old Testament is a bony fish. But so is the New Testament.)

Whether Jesus is historical, fictional, or a combination of both, I consider myself a student in the school of Jesus. Or, as I like to call it, "the school of love," from which there may be dropouts but no graduates. After all, learning how to love never ends. I'm not sure what it means to "follow Jesus" as many born-again and evangelical Christians put it. But I do know what it means to be a student in a vocational school of love that continues to grow and adapt to times and circumstance. In that school students learn to be ecumenical, not exclusive or elitist. And as far as I can tell, whatever this Christian thing is, it's an extension of Judaism, not a replacement, as the gospels themselves show.

Four gospels tell the "official" story of Jesus—the gospel according to Matthew, the gospel according to Mark, the gospel according to Luke, and the gospel according to John. *According to*—which is to say, the story of Jesus from a certain perspective. (A dozen or so other gospels were not included in the New Testament canon. But that's a story for another day.)

Most scholars agree that Mark was published first (ca. 70 CE). Later, Matthew (ca. 85 CE) and Luke (ca. 90 CE) built their own amended and expanded versions on Mark's foundation. Those three gospels are known collectively as "the synoptic gospels," because they share a similar narrative structure. (*Syn* "similar"; *optic* means "view.")

The gospel according to John developed independently of those three and was published much later (ca. 110 CE). It has a different narrative structure.

The school (or schools) of Jesus used grist from his life and teachings along with some poetic license to create the gospels. They turned a minor figure into a legend. Again, not unusual then or even now.

So how much of the real, historical Jesus is depicted accurately in the gospels? No one knows. But it really doesn't matter. At least not to me. Of course, there's nothing wrong with probing underneath the gospel texts (a kind of excavation) to locate the historical Jesus, to distinguish his actual words and deeds from presumptive ones. For some people that's important. That's how we got versions of the Bible with Jesus's words highlighted in red. But were they actually his words or made up by his sect?

*Who is the historical Jesus? Did Jesus really say that? Did Jesus really do that?*

The theologian David Strauss (1808–74) pioneered the search for the historical Jesus in his *Life of Jesus* (1835). He reputedly applied unbiased historical methods and rejected all supernatural events as mythical. More biographies of Jesus would ensue, including Albert Schweitzer's popular *Quest for the Historical Jesus* (1906). That quest has continued in various permutations to the present—probing for the "real Jesus" beneath the pages of the New Testament.

But by reading the gospels as sectarian tracts, we avoid that question. We simply accept the canonical Jesus as portrayed in the text. If we have issues with the gospels, it is not with Jesus per se; it is with those who wrote and edited the gospels. It's as though Jesus were a prop in their promotional pamphlets.

How did the various gospels come about?

Imagine a group of Americans who worked with Martin Luther King in the 1960s. Imagine their shock after his assassination in April 1968.

Imagine that his friends and supporters determine to carry on his work and to draw others into the movement by enshrining his words, deeds, and vision in stories about him. Now imagine that no one had access to audio, video, or print records—just memories. Imagine those stories conveyed orally for forty years before various authorized written versions ("according to") appeared for the first time in 2018. From 1968 to 2018 is forty years.

The first written gospel appeared forty years after the death of Jesus (ca. 30 CE). King and Jesus lived in different times, in different circumstances, but each was canonized over a period of forty years.

The story of Jesus—his words, deeds, and vision—is enshrined in the gospels. The story is devotional, mystical, transcendental, and transformative. It has warmed and revived the hearts of countless people who have no doubt whatsoever that Jesus is real. He walks and talks with them. He's by their side, in their hearts, and in their hymns.

"Jesus Is the Sweetest Name I Know." "What a Friend We Have in Jesus." "Jesu, Joy of Man's Desiring." "Jesus, Lover of My Soul."

That's devotional language. It's not meant to be measured and weighed for accuracy or intellectual content. It's how lovers talk about their beloved. *You are so beautiful to me, the most beautiful person in the world!* No one's going to demand proof. We understand and accept how lovers talk.

Countless multitudes believe in Jesus as their Lord and Savior. I once did too. But, then, I also once believed in Santa. I believed he was as real as my Uncle Rufus. I believed Santa was historical, not fictional. I was a true believer from age two until age seven.

And then I found out.

I learned that Santa wasn't real. The whole thing was a myth. Fiction. So I (reluctantly) put away that childish faith. No one tried to stop me. No one disparaged my decision. It was the socially acceptable thing to do at my age. If I hadn't, twelve-year-olds would have ridiculed me to death.

But real or not, Santa made me happy. Santa kept hope alive. He filled my heart with joy and wonder (and a little fear). He kept an eye on me. He knew where I lived. I had a "personal relationship" with him.

At that age I also believed in Jesus, but he wasn't as real to me as he was to my parents. I'd never sat on his lap or wrote him a letter. In the case of Jesus, I was told to pray, which, I must admit, felt like talking to myself.

But Santa heard me, read my letters, and delivered. Santa was real.

Like the Jesus myth, the Santa Claus myth was inspired by an actual, historical person. The Santa myth grew from Saint Nicholas of Myra, who lived in the fourth century. He was known for his kindness and charity. He gave children gifts.

The Santa legend was embellished by the Dutch (who called him Sinterklaas), brought over to New Amsterdam (New York), memorialized in 1863 by the *Harper's Weekly* cartoonist Thomas Nast, whose illustration was inspired by the poem "Twas the Night Before Christmas," first published anonymously in 1823. In 1931 Coca-Cola introduced a jolly Santa with rosy cheeks, a white beard, and twinkling eyes. The myth was celebrated in songs, stories, and movies.

Santa makes a good story. It resonates with children. Facts don't matter. Children happily believe. Adults play along.

The Jesus story is also largely myth. Many believe it. Some play along. Others dismiss it as childish. But real or not, the Jesus story makes people happy. It keeps hope alive. It fills hearts with joy and wonder.

The Jesus presented in the gospels, in hymns, and art evokes adulation from many people who seek to emulate his life, to love and serve others in his name. And that's a good thing. I hope nothing said in this book undermines such love of and service to others inspired by Jesus.

Still, no one knows what Jesus actually said or did. The redactors of the four canonical gospels did with the figure of Jesus what previous Jewish writers did with the legendary figures of Moses, Elijah, David, Ruth, and Esther. They embellished and embroidered.

In other words, when it came to sacred writing, the gospel redactors had models to emulate. They mythologized history. The historical Jesus was lost under countless emendations.

In 1985 Robert Funk founded "the Jesus Seminars." Panelists graded the sayings of Jesus in the gospels from "most likely" to "very unlikely" with gradient colors. It was a tedious but fascinating exercise. It drew media attention and public interest but also scorn and denunciations. The findings from those seminars are available on the Westar Institute website.

I respect those efforts, but I don't see what they get us. Does one grade of sayings trump the others? Who decides? Besides, what does it matter if "love your enemies" or "welcome the outcast" or "feed the hungry" came from a historical Jesus, a canonical Jesus, from his school, or from his mother?

It's what's said, not who says it that matters. Usually.

Regardless of whether Socrates said "Know thyself," it's good advice. And the same goes for Jesus and "Love your neighbor." It's good advice. And it was said long before Jesus said it.

🍎 🍎 🍎

# CHAPTER 16

# How the Hebrew Scriptures
# Shaped the Gospels

The gospels are not biographies. Typically, biographies include accounts of the subject's childhood, youth, family, friends, mentors, and influences. The gospels contain nothing on those matters except a brief birth narrative in Matthew and Luke and a brief snapshot of Jesus in Jerusalem at age twelve. Each gospel focuses on three years of Jesus's life, from age thirty to thirty-three. Three years is not enough for a biography.

The stories about Jesus are similar to the stories about other historical figures (Confucius, Genghis Khan, Julius Caesar, Buddha, Mohammed, Frances of Assisi, Joan of Arc, Napoleon)—narratives that embellish and canonize a mortal life. We may be informed, edified, and inspired by those stories, but still we take them with a grain of salt. There's no reason not to do the same with the gospels.

So what are the gospels if not biographies? Are they like any known literary genre of that time?

Yes, they are.

The redactors of the gospels didn't have to look far to find models. They'd read or heard the legendary stories of Abraham, Moses, Joshua, and Elijah. Those stories were precedents for the gospel narratives.

In Matthew, Jesus is presented as another Moses, delivering new laws from a mountain as Moses had done, according to the book of Exodus. In Luke, Jesus is presented as another Elijah, feeding the hungry, confronting authorities, and raising the dead as Elijah had done, according to the book of First Kings. And like Elijah, Jesus was raptured into heaven. (Acts 1.6–11) In John, Jesus is presented as the Creator's eternal, playful feminine partner (Sophia or Wisdom), existing before creation, according to Proverbs.

The gospels are refractions, not reflections of Jesus—like a view through a prism rather than a window. Not only did Jesus teach in parables, but the gospels themselves may be seen respectively as four extended parables composed out of his life.

Below is a list of eight venerable images, figures, and stories from the Hebrew scriptures the redactors consciously or unconsciously drew on to shape the life of Jesus. By appropriating themes and tropes from their venerable scriptures, they show Jesus as a reformer within a heritage, not as an innovator. "I have come to fulfill the law, not to abolish it." (Matthew 5.17) On the Mount of Transfiguration (Matthew 17.1–3), Jesus stands with Moses and Elijah. It doesn't get more venerable (or Jewish) than that!

1. **Isaac.** In obedience to an order from God, Abraham led his son Isaac on a journey to Mount Moriah with the intent to sacrifice (kill!) him on an altar. Abraham carried a dagger; Isaac carried wood on his shoulder. (Genesis 22.1–19) The wooden cross that Jesus carried on his shoulder up another mount, the mount of Calvary harks back to the wood that Isaac lugged.

    Isaac was an obedient "beloved son" even unto death. It's as though Isaac said to his father as Jesus did to his: "Not my will but thine be done." (Luke 22.42)

    Isaac was spared. He rose from the pyre, left the mount, and eventually procreated a people as numerous as the stars. (Genesis 17.4) Following his resurrection, Jesus created a "people of many nations." (Matthew 28.28)

2. **Joseph.** Joseph was a beloved son. His father, Jacob, gave him a coat of many colors. Jesus was a beloved son as well. According to the baptism narrative in Mark, Jesus heard a voice from heaven say: *You are my beloved, with you I am well pleased!* (Mark 1.8)

    Joseph was betrayed by his brothers, specifically by Judah. (Genesis 37.26–28) Jesus was betrayed by Judas. (Matthew 26.14–16) The betrayers have the same root name.

The betrayal of Joseph landed him in Egypt as a slave. Eventually he ascended to become the minister of agriculture—from tragedy to glory. According to Joseph the evil act of betrayal by his brothers unwittingly saved the world, including his family, from a severe famine. *You meant it for evil; but God meant it for good.* (Genesis 50.20) Joseph's suffering saved the world.

The betrayal of Jesus landed him in the hands of the Romans. He was tried, tortured, and crucified. But like Joseph, Jesus ascended from tragedy to glory. He ascended into heaven. Jesus's suffering, it is said, saved the world.

3. **Moses.** Moses delivered a set of laws and instructions from a mountain in order to constitute a nation out of a motley bunch of undisciplined former slaves. He aimed to instill and cultivate certain attitudes, behaviors, and aspirations in them. *Do not murder, lie, or covet,* and so on. (Exodus 12)

   Jesus delivered a set of laws and directives from a mountain to constitute a certain kind of people with certain attitudes, behaviors, and aspirations. *Give alms. Love your enemies. Bless those who curse you. You are the salt of the earth, the light of the world.* (Matthew 5–7)

4. **Joshua.** Joshua selected twelve "mighty men of valor" (one from each of the twelve tribes of Israel) to lead the conquest of Canaan with swords. (Joshua 3.12) Jesus selected twelve men. Unlike Joshua's team, Jesus's team was not particularly known for valor or skills with a sword. (Luke 6.1) But they numbered twelve, symbolic of the founding twelve tribes from which Joshua selected. (Ten tribes were "lost" following the Assyrian conquest of northern Israel in the eighth century BCE.) Twelve symbolized an aspiration to make Israel whole again, arousing hope and expectation among the Jews.

   Joshua surveyed the land to plan a bloody invasion. A thousand years later Jesus surveyed the same land to plan a campaign of compassion for the sick, the hungry, the outcast, and the tormented. Joshua wielded a sword. Jesus wielded the servant's towel. That's a sharp contrast, a discontinuity. Yet

Joshua and Jesus are the same Hebrew name (Yeshua) spelled differently.

5. **King David.** David defeated his enemies and built a glorious nation out of twelve disparate tribes. He united the northern and southern tribes into one kingdom. Jesus aimed to establish a glorious kingdom out of disparate nations: *I tell you, many will come from east and west and will take their places at the banquet with Abraham and Isaac and Jacob in the kingdom of heaven.* (Matthew 8.11) David was called "the son of God."

6. **Elijah.** In Luke, Jesus is presented as another Elijah, manipulating the weather, feeding the hungry, confronting authorities, and raising the dead—as Elijah did, according to the book of First Kings.

   Elijah was raptured into the clouds (heaven) while his disciple Elisha looked on. (2 Kings 2.11–12) Jesus was raptured into the clouds while his disciples looked on. (Acts 1.9) Elijah's mantle fell upon his disciple Elisha so he could continue Elijah's work. Jesus's spirit fell upon his disciples so they could continue his work. Elijah ascended in a fiery chariot. Soon after Jesus ascended, tongues as of fire appeared over the heads of the disciples. (Acts 2.1–4)

7. **Jonah.** Jonah spent three days in the belly of a big fish (a watery grave) before emerging to undertake his mission of grace to the inhabitants of Nineveh, Israel's notorious and powerful enemy. Jesus spent three days in an earthen grave before emerging with a message of grace for the inhabitants of the whole world: *Go into all the world, proclaiming salvation to all.* (Matthew 28.28, paraphrased)

8. **Daniel.** The book of Daniel is a subversive political tract in the guise of a dream. (Daniel 7) In his vision Daniel saw the destruction of four brutal, beastly kingdoms (depicted as a lion, an eagle, a leopard, and a dragon) that had previously oppressed the Jewish people including the one in Daniel's time—Greece. Following the appearance of these monstrous beasts of prey, Daniel saw one like "the son of man," a human one descending

from the clouds to establish a new kingdom, a humane empire, on earth.

In the gospels Jesus frequently identified himself as "the son of man" but never as the "son of God." "Son of man" can simply refer to the one speaking, like saying "yours truly." But "son of man" may also have intentionally evoked Daniel's dream and with it the prospects of a humane governance on earth. After all, Jesus proclaimed the empire of heaven as a replacement for the empire of Rome. Rome barely noticed. At first. The Jesus of the gospels was not only a teacher and healer, he was also an apocalyptic preacher of the *eschaton* (the final event in the divine plan) as noted by Schweitzer.

All these allusions would have been obvious to first-century Jews but not so much to us unless we've read the Old Testament extensively.

These stories, tropes, and figures were available to the novel sect as it shaped the life and teachings of Jesus in narrative form for a Jewish audience. The narrative was shaped by writers. And writers, like all artists, stand on the shoulders of their predecessors and consciously or unconsciously draw on their work. The gospels were written by creative and passionate writers. They made Jesus real.

# CHAPTER 17

# A Gospel Older Than "the Gospels"

N one of the four gospels were initially called gospels. Furthermore, they were published anonymously. Not until the second century were the familiar titles—the gospel according to Matthew, Mark, Luke, John—affixed to them.

As the New Testament scholar Bart Ehrman puts it, "Contrary to what you may sometimes have heard, there is no concrete evidence that the Gospels received their familiar names early on. It is absolutely true to say that in the manuscripts of the Gospels, they have the titles we are accustomed to. But these manuscripts with titles do not start appearing until around 200 CE. What were manuscripts of, say, Matthew or John entitled in the year 120 CE? We have no way of knowing. The titles almost certainly cannot be what the authors themselves called their works." (*The Bart Ehrman Blog*, November 17, 2014)

Why, then, did they become known as the gospels?

The word *gospel* (good news) is prominent in the book of Isaiah, published six hundred years before the New Testament employed it. The gospel of Mark begins: *The beginning of the gospel of Jesus Christ, the Son of God.* (Mark 1.1)

Next comes a citation from Isaiah, chapter 40: *As it is written in the prophet Isaiah "Behold, I am sending my messenger ahead of you who will prepare your way; the voice of one crying out in the wilderness: Prepare the way of the Lord, make his paths straight."*

That passage introduces John the Baptist as the messenger who prepares the way for Jesus. In other words, Mark presents the life of John and Jesus with backlighting from Isaiah.

Mark announces the *beginning* of the gospel *of Jesus Christ,* not the beginning of *the gospel,* per se. Six hundred years earlier there had been a gospel "according to Isaiah" or, possibly, according to the "school of Isaiah." The brief citation in Mark ("Behold, I am sending my messenger . . .") was enough of a cue for most Jewish readers or listeners to recall the verses that followed, the way the words "We hold these truths to be self-evident" call to mind for many Americans the full text of the Declaration of Independence, or the way "O, say, can you see" calls to mind the entire "Star-Spangled Banner." Jews were weaned and raised on their scriptures. It was their daily bread. So when a Jewish audience heard "Behold, I am sending my messenger," the words below instantly came to mind.

> *Get you up to a high mountain,*
> *O Zion, herald of GOOD TIDINGS;*
> *lift up your voice with strength,*
> *O Jerusalem, herald of GOOD TIDING,*
> *lift it up, do not fear;*
> *say to the cities of Judah,*
> *"Here is your God!"*

> *How beautiful upon the mountains*
> *are the feet of the messenger who announces peace,*
> *who brings GOOD NEWS,*
> *who announces salvation,*
> *who says to Zion, "Your God reigns."*
> (Isaiah 40.9, emphasis added)

The school of Jesus reintroduced a gospel first annunciated by Isaiah. There's more.

> *The spirit of the Lord God is upon me,*
> *because the Lord has anointed me;*
> *he has sent me to bring GOOD NEWS to the oppressed,*
> *to bind up the brokenhearted,*
> *to proclaim liberty to the captives,*
> *and release to the prisoners;*
> *to proclaim the year of the Lord's favor,*
> *and the day of vengeance of our God;*
> *to comfort all who mourn;*
> *to provide for those who mourn in Zion—*
> *to give them a garland instead of ashes,*

*the oil of gladness instead of mourning,*
*the mantle of praise instead of a faint spirit.*
(Isaiah 61.1–3, emphasis added)

The above passage was cited by Jesus (with the notable omission of "the day of vengeance") when he announced his mission in a synagogue in Nazareth: *The spirit of the Lord is upon me for he has anointed me to proclaim good news.* (Luke 4.18) In other words, Isaiah's old gospel became the marching orders, the agenda, of a new sect. The gospel of Jesus.

One other possible source for the use of the word *gospel* comes from Roman society. The Romans considered Augustus's reign as gospel (Greek *evangelion*) or "good news" as seen in an edict proclaimed in 9 BCE and inscribed in stone. It was discovered in Priene in Western Turkey and thus is known as the Priene Calendar. It is preserved in the Berlin Museum in Germany. The citation below is taken from Wikipedia.

*Since Providence, which has ordered all things and is deeply interested in our life, has set in most perfect order by giving us Augustus, whom she filled with virtue that he might benefit humankind, sending him as a SAVIOR, both for us and for our descendants, THAT HE MIGHT END WAR and arrange all things, and since he, Caesar, by his appearance (excelled even our anticipations), surpassing all previous benefactors, and not even leaving to posterity any hope of surpassing what he has done, and since the birthday of the god Augustus was THE BEGINNING OF THE GOOD TIDINGS [εὐαγγέλιον, i.e, evangelion, gospel] for the world that came by reason of him."* (emphasis added)

(That, by the way, is devotional language.)

It's possible that the New Testament gospels were composed not only with Isaiah's gospel in mind but also the well-publicized gospel of the god Augustus in mind. *The beginning of the gospel of Jesus Christ* versus *the beginning of the gospel of Augustus.* Heralds (evangelists) proclaimed the gospel of Augustus throughout the empire. Rome had its evangelists. The Jesus sect did too.

The evangelists from the "school of Jesus" presented Jesus as the true emperor. Jesus, not Augustus, is "the son of God." The kingdom of God is the true kingdom. Rome's is not. Augustus is not the real "Prince of Peace." Jesus is.

As Marcus Borg put it, it was a "battle of myths."

*You have your gospel. We have ours. Let the contest begin. Whose kingdom will reign forever and ever?*

Come and follow me, Jesus says. Join our movement and you will learn that the power of love is greater than the power of the sword. In our school, love is the curriculum.

*Love your neighbor as yourself. Love your enemies. Do unto others as you would have them do unto you.*

Ask almost anyone about Jesus, and they'll tell you he taught and practiced love. As it turns out, many people detest Christianity (or what we might call "Churchianity")—what with its notorious emphasis on original sin and eternal punishment in hell—but they like Jesus. He was fully human. He revealed humanity's capacity to love.

But in the fourth century Jesus nearly lost his humanity to Mary's virginity.

# CHAPTER 18

# Was Jesus Born of a Virgin?

*An angel of the Lord appeared to Joseph in a dream and said, "Joseph, son of David, do not be afraid to take Mary as your wife, for the child conceived in her is from the Holy Spirit. She will bear a son, and you are to name him Jesus, for he will save his people from their sins." All this took place to fulfill what had been spoken by the Lord through the prophet:*

> *"Look, the VIRGIN shall become pregnant and give birth to a son,*
> *and they shall name him Emmanuel,*
> *which means, 'God is with us.'"*

(Matthew 1.20–23, emphasis added)

🍎 🍎 🍎

The angel's message ends with a citation from the prophet Isaiah. ("The virgin shall become pregnant.") By now we know how the Hebrew scriptures backlight much of the gospels. So it no surprise to hear the angel cite the prophet Isaiah. What is surprising is that the angel (according to Matthew) says "virgin" when the Isaiah says "young woman."

*Then Isaiah said, "Hear then, O house of David! Is it too little for you to weary mortals that you weary my God also? Therefore the Lord himself will give you a sign. Look, a YOUNG WOMAN is with child and shall bear a son and shall name him Immanuel." (Isaiah 7.13–14, emphasis added)*

So before we get to the substantial part of the nativity story (the naming of Jesus), let's sidetrack this virgin "sideshow." (The virgin birth is mentioned nowhere else in the New Testament except once in Luke. The disciples and the apostle Paul seem to know nothing of it. It was not officially a big deal until the fourth century.)

Matthew transports his readers back to Isaiah's prophetic assurance of deliverance for a beleaguered Israel in the seventh century BCE in order to bolster the Jewish people in the present—another dark time in the land.

*A young woman is pregnant. A child shall be born. Life goes on, people. God is with us. As always.*

Wittingly or unwittingly, Matthew replaced Isaiah's Hebrew word for "young women" (*almah*) with the Greek word for "virgin" (*parthenos*). It became a ticking time bomb. A few centuries later that mistranslation became fodder for Mary's literal virginity. Her virginity became a creedal test of orthodox Christian faith as found in the Apostles' Creed (ca. 340 CE).

*I believe in God the Father Almighty, Maker of heaven and earth. And in Jesus Christ, His only Son, our Lord; Who was conceived by the Holy Spirit; Born of the Virgin Mary.*

Why did Matthew substitute "virgin" for "young woman"?

He didn't.

It was in the translation he referenced.

Matthew (and many other Jews) read the Hebrew scriptures in the widely available Greek translation known as the Septuagint. Translations, then as now, are seldom precise word-to-word equivalences. So translating *almah* as *parthenos* is not that remarkable. It doesn't indicate fraudulence. The translators didn't have gynecology in mind.

(*Almah. Parthenos. Close enough. Next sentence.*)

Now to the more substantial part of the nativity story.

Was Jesus born of a virgin?

No. The gospels say he was. But that's fiction.

Was his mother impregnated by God?

No. The gospels say she was. But that's fiction.

Did Jesus have a natural father?

Yes.

Was it Joseph?

No.

Does anyone know who the biological father was?

No. But there was a rumor. More on that later.

Jesus's contemporaries assumed Jesus had a natural father. *All spoke well of him and were amazed at the gracious words that came from his mouth. They said, "Is this not Joseph's son?"* (Luke 4.22) They weren't stupid. They knew the laws of nature. A woman claiming to have conceived a baby without sexual intercourse would be deemed a boldface liar or completely naive.

Mary was pregnant. Everyone could see that. Mary was unmarried. Everyone knew that. And everyone knew it was scandalous.

We don't know whether Mary ever said who the natural father was, but Joseph clearly knew it wasn't him. If Mary had claimed impregnation by the Holy Spirit, Joseph would have laughed scornfully. He was no fool. He planned to ban her for breaking their betrothal vows and shaming him. But he changed his mind, as we shall see.

First, let's consider the rumor.

A rumor appeared early and persisted at least into the mid-second century that Jesus's father was a Roman soldier. Celsus, a second-century Greek philosopher, made that claim, which drew this response from Origen, an early Christian apologist, in his work *Against Celsus* (ca. 248 CE).

*Let us return, however, to the words put into the mouth of the Jew, where "the mother of Jesus" is described as having been "turned out by the carpenter who was betrothed to her, as she had been convicted of adultery and had a child by a certain soldier named Panthera."*

That's not much to base a controversial theory on since Celsus's claim is not known outside Origen's reference to it. Still, it establishes that there was a rumor of a soldier's role in Mary's impregnation.

That rumor had credibility. After all, it is far easier to believe that a Roman soldier impregnated Mary than to believe there was no father whatsoever. First-century Jews might have believed in angels, demons, and manna from heaven, but they did not believe a woman could conceive without a man's contribution.

The existence of Panthera or any other paternal candidate has never been verified. Still, it is not out of the realm of possibility, knowing how occupying forces—then and now—treat subjected women. As shocking as that sounds in the wake of Mary's sanctification, it makes more sense than believing a human egg was fertilized without a human sperm. That doesn't happen—except in myths. And there, it happens quite often.

Still, there was something remarkable about Jesus's nativity that is lost in the squabbles over virginity.

*Now the birth of Jesus the Messiah took place in this way. When his mother Mary had been engaged to Joseph, but before they lived together, she was found to be pregnant from the Holy Spirit. Her husband Joseph, being a righteous man and unwilling to expose her to public disgrace, planned to divorce her quietly.* (Matthew 1.18–19)

While contemplating divorce, Joseph—like his Old Testament namesake Joseph, the renowned dreamer (wink, wink)—had a dream. And just like that, Joseph changed his mind.

*Joseph took Mary as his wife but had no marital relations with her until she had given birth to a son, and he named him Jesus.* (Matthew 1.24–25)

Although many may have regarded Jesus as "illegitimate," his parents did not. Despite his dubious paternity, Mary and Joseph embraced Jesus because Mary and Joseph were good and faithful Jews. They knew the law of Moses about welcoming the stranger, the outsider, the neglected. Thus, the public naming of a "bastard child" was a radical, compassionate act. The "marginalized one" was fully included. And that's a critical part of the nativity story.

And so it is no surprise that Jesus accepted and embraced those whom society rejected or marginalized as illegitimate, unworthy of respect. Like his parents, Jesus defied social norms in the name of compassion. Jesus was a good and faithful Jew. He associated with "deplorable" people.

# CHAPTER 19

# Did Jesus Die for Our Sins?

*For I handed on to you as of first importance what I in turn had received: that Christ died for our sins in accordance with the scriptures.* (1 Corinthians 15.3)

🍎 🍎 🍎

Did Jesus really die on the cross *for our sins*? I'll get to that, but let's begin with an easier question: Did Jesus die on a cross?

Probably.

The Romans crucified thousands of alleged or confirmed rebels and insurrectionists. So the death of Jesus by crucifixion is completely within the realm of historical probabilities.

Did Jesus die for our sins?

That's a different sort of question. To say he did requires an extrapolation from his death that cannot be verified by mere observation.

We could have seen Jesus on the cross. We could have seen the nails, the oozing blood, the last breath. But we could not have *seen* that he died for our sins (whatever that means) without a certain particular lens.

To believe that Jesus "died for our sins" takes a cluster of interlocking ideas regarding sin, blood sacrifices, and the necessity to appease an offended, angry deity. Such a cluster existed in Hebrew scripture.

Actually, the sacrifice of animals or humans to appease the gods once made sense in the ancient Aztec and Roman worlds, as well as the Jewish. But not in the world of their descendants.

And yet the requirement of sacrifice to atone for sins still makes sense to many Christians today. They swear by it. The church teaches it to children. As a child, I learned to sing: "What can wash away my sins? Nothing but the blood of Jesus!" Children still sing that in Sunday School classes.

As you know, first impressions are lasting impressions. Consequently, many adults never outgrow that first impression. They live in a bygone era of angry gods and bloody sacrifices to atone for sin.

They don't have to, but they do.

You can reject the invention of motorized vehicles and drive Amish buggies. But you don't have to.

You can reject vaccines and take your chances. But you don't have to.

You can reject advanced therapy, surgery, and medication. But you don't have to.

You can reject the idea that God is love (or the idea that there is no God to appease) and cower in fear of eternal damnation. But you don't have to.

Did Jesus die for the sins of the world?

No.

Jesus died because the Roman Empire considered him a threat to its world domination. Jesus offered an alternative kingdom, a world without violence or discrimination. He rallied a following. His following grew. He prophesied the end of the (Roman) world and the resurrection of a new world. He gave oppressed people hope. He gave the empire chills.

Jesus didn't die *for* the sins of the world. But we might say he died *because* of the sins of the world, specifically the sins of the Roman Empire—greed, oppression, and injustice.

If Jesus had been hanged for insurrection in nineteenth-century America, few, if any, Americans would have taken his death as first-century Jews and proto-Christians took it. The cluster of ideas regarding sin and bloody sacrifice no longer obtained in the nineteenth American culture. A different understanding of reality obtained.

(But, let's say, some nineteenth-century Christians did perceive his death as atonement for sin. Would they wear miniature ornamental nooses around their necks as many Christians now wear ornamental crosses? Just sayin'.)

Abraham Lincoln, Gandhi, and Martin Luther King Jr. died as martyrs. They were idolized and lionized. But no one claims their deaths appeased God's wrath, remitted sins, and atoned for individual and collective guilt. Our cluster of ideas supports a political, not a theological, interpretation of their deaths.

Jesus was a martyr. The blood of martyrs waters the seeds of justice and raises up a company of people determined to bend the arc of the universe toward justice.

Something arose in the wake of Jesus's death.

# CHAPTER 20

# Was Jesus Resurrected?

Did Jesus come back to life three days after his crucifixion?

No, according to the laws of nature.

Yes, according to the apostle Paul.

*Christ died for our sins in accordance with the scriptures. He was buried and was raised on the third day in accordance with the scriptures. He appeared to Cephas, then to the twelve. Then he appeared to more than five hundred brothers and sisters at one time, most of whom are still alive, though some have died. Then he appeared to James, then to all the apostles. Last of all, as to one untimely born, he appeared also to me.* (1 Corinthians 15.3–8)

Did Jesus come back to life three days after his crucifixion?

No, according to the laws of nature.

Yes, according to the gospels.

*While they were talking about this, Jesus himself stood among them and said to them, "Peace be with you." They were startled and terrified and thought that they were seeing a ghost. He said to them, "Why are you frightened, and why do doubts arise in your hearts? Look at my hands and my feet; see that it is I myself. Touch me and see, for a ghost does not have flesh and bones as you see that I have."*

*And when he had said this, he showed them his hands and his feet. Yet for all their joy they were still disbelieving and wondering, and he said to them, "Have you anything here to eat?" They gave him a piece of broiled fish, and he took it and ate in their presence.* (Luke 24.36–42)

I know there are many things about this world we don't know and may never know. After all, laws are derived from probabilities, not absolutes. So, logically, anything is possible even if highly improbable. There's a gap between high probability and absolute certainty. We get over the gap with a leap of faith.

Still, I can't believe the resurrection of Jesus as the gospels present it. I side with natural law. Dead bodies do not come back to life. (Or, so says my "faith.") I can, however, accept that many people had a mystical experience of Jesus after his death. Mystical experiences are real. The resurrection was real to them, as real as real can be. Not everything real is physical.

*We saw him. We heard him. We touched him.*

I don't disregard their experience. But, then, experiences are one thing; expressions of experiences are something else.

If a bereaved widow says her deceased husband appeared to her in the flesh, spoke audibly, and embraced her, we wouldn't believe it. Why? Because dead bodies do not come back to life.

Whether it was mystical or apparitional, it was real to the widow. And the only way to express her nonverbal mystical experience was with ordinary words. We may disregard her depiction ("He was really there!") but not her experience ("I felt great peace."). Only an unsympathetic person would dispute the widow and demand empirical evidence.

Mystical experiences are real.

The apostle Paul described his mystical encounter with the resurrected Jesus as an "appearance" (apparition, perhaps) without any physical attributions other than a voice. Jesus did not invite Paul to touch him as he did others—"doubting" Thomas, for example. Nor did Paul see a body as Mary did in the garden or as two disciples did on the road to Emmaus.

But then Paul was a mystic. He said that he had once been transported into "the third heaven" and "into paradise"—in or out of body, he couldn't tell—seeing "visions and revelations." (2 Corinthians 12.14)

Paul was a mystic.

Paul heard a bodiless Jesus speak ("an appearance"), while the witnesses in the gospel saw a bodily Jesus. (Interestingly, Paul also referred to those sightings as "appearances," which means he considered those "physical sightings" on a par with the nonphysical "appearance" of Jesus.) Experiences are one thing; expressions of experiences are something else.

It's unlikely that Paul was the only mystic among the followers of Jesus.

As with other stories in the gospels, the resurrection story was refracted through Hebrew texts. As Paul wrote in 50 CE: Jesus was dead, buried, and raised on the third day, *according to the scriptures.* (1 Corinthians 15.4, emphasis added)

Jesus wasn't just raised. He was raised *according to the scriptures.* According to *what* scriptures?

Not the New Testament scriptures. There were none in 50 CE. The earliest gospel (Mark) wasn't published until about 70 CE. Paul wrote the above passage twenty years before Mark and about twenty years after the crucifixion—before there were any official Christian scriptures.

*Jesus was dead, buried, and raised on the third day, according to the scriptures.*

What scriptures?

It can only be the Hebrew scriptures.

As it turns out, several ancient Hebrew texts anticipated and described a *bodily* resurrection long before Jesus. Those passages likely shaped the telling of the resurrection stories.

For example, five hundred years *before* Jesus, the poet-prophet Ezekiel foresaw a "valley of dry bones" (symbolizing the "dead"—or as good-as-dead—people of the Jewish nation) revivified. In his vision the dry bones reassembled, stood up, and breathed. A mighty host of reborn people. Though crushed and trampled into the dust by Babylon, the Jewish people would rise up again, or so Ezekiel believed. (Ezekiel 37)

That's *bodily* resurrection. It's flesh and bones. It's also nationalistic (the whole nation) not individualistic (one person)—a corporate not a personal resurrection. Maybe "Jesus" was seen as a prologue for a greater resurrection yet to come. Could be. As we know, the scriptures allow for multiple interpretations.

The Romans crushed Jesus like the Babylonians had crushed Israel, but he rose up like those bones in Ezekiel's dry valley. Reborn. Alive in the flesh.

As we saw earlier, Judaism is a body-affirming tradition. According to Genesis 1, the material world and all therein, including human bodies, are called "good" and "blessed." (Genesis 1) The body is not something to escape as it is in Greek philosophy. There, the soul is trapped inside a body like a hand in a glove. The glove is evil, corrupt. Leave it behind! That's salvation in the Greek world of thought.

Not so in Judaism. Hand and glove are one. Both are good. Keep them together. They are inseparable anyway. (The Hebrew word often translated "soul" is *nephesh, which* means "breath" or "being." Soul is not a separate entity, at least not in early Judaism.) Thus, "Bless the Lord, O my soul" (Psalm 103.1) is more accurate as, "Bless the Lord, all my being."

All this is to say that if a resurrection story were to be believed within the Jewish milieu of the first century, it would have to be flesh and blood, not a ghost, not soul survival. A Greek-type spiritual resurrection was not in the cards (or we could say, not in the scriptures).

Jesus's body did not rise, but another body did—a body of people imbued with his spirit, his character, his passion, his compassion—not unlike the body of people who rose up in the wake of Gandhi's and Martin Luther King's assassinations and even in the wake of John Brown's hanging.

*John Brown's body lies a-moldering in the grave, but his soul goes marching on.*

Can the gospel text bear such an interpretation?

I think so.

The apostle Paul employed a metaphor for the resurrection that unwittingly supports my interpretation. I say "unwittingly" because I'm not sure Paul intended the metaphor to be taken as I take it.

*But someone will ask, "How are the dead raised? With what kind of body do they come?" Fool! What you sow does not come to life unless it dies. And as for what you sow, you do not sow the body that is to be but a bare seed, perhaps of wheat or of some other grain. But God gives it a body as he has chosen and to each kind of seed its own body.* (1 Corinthians 15.35–38)

When you plant an acorn, you don't expect a bigger acorn to rise from the ground. You expect an oak tree. The body of Jesus went into the earth. The body of Jesus did not come out of the earthen grave. Something else emerged—a bold, brave, dynamic community teaching and practicing love, justice, and mercy for all.

As the international human rights activist Reverend Erica Williams, put it:

*A man considered a nobody set [a movement] off by showing radical love and revolutionary compassion and by speaking truth to power. Jesus turned the world right side up. The empire thought it had shut Jesus down by lynching him, but all it did was plant a seed.*

*That seed has produced a great harvest of freedom fighters such as Harriet Tubman, Frederick Douglass, Fannie Lou Hamer, Ella Josephine Baker, Septima Clark, and Martin Luther King Jr. Each of us is being called to set it off. It does not matter what your pedigree is: God is calling you to stand for truth and justice.* (Erica N. Williams, *We Cry Justice*, 2021)

Yes. Amen. But let's not get carried away here. The resurrected community of Jesus practices compassion, justice, and radical hospitality—until it doesn't. It dies and rises again—continually.

Many people believe the resurrection of Jesus's body is literal and thus indisputable proof that he is the one and only true son of God. He wasn't merely resuscitated, they say, he was resurrected with a new and transcendent body.

Such people believe the resurrection makes Christianity *superior* to all other religions because no other religion has *that*. (Well, maybe no other "religion" does, but other cultures do have tales of resurrected beings: Egyptian [Osiris], Norse [Odin], Aztec [Quetzalcóatl], to name a few.)

Many Christians believe that the resurrection *proves* that Jesus is the true Messiah while all other claimants are false or pretenders since only Jesus and no other has been raised physically from death. Unfortunately, such a belief makes many Christians arrogant and judgmental.

*Believe it and you'll go to heaven like me. Deny it and you'll go to hell.*

Well, I believe in the resurrection. I just don't believe the resurrection of Jesus as a physical fact. I believe it as a spiritual fact.

And I'm in good company.

A physical resurrection wasn't necessary for Leo Tolstoy, Albert Schweitzer, or Gandhi to follow Jesus's moral teaching and exemplary life. They believed in the way of Jesus without believing in a bodily resurrection.

And I'll go so far as to say Jesus would agree. A resurrection adds nothing to his message and mission. As he himself said, "If they ignore Moses and the prophets, they will not listen even should one return from the dead." (Luke 16.31)

That quotation is from a parable Jesus told about a rich man, Dives, and a beggar, Lazarus, who sat at the rich man's gate every day. Dives ignored Lazarus and withheld aid.

Both died.

Dives went to Hades. Lazarus to the bosom of Abraham. Dives was in torment but could see across the great divide that Lazarus was blissfully comfortable. Dives begged Abraham to send Lazarus to warn Dives's five brothers not to do as he had done lest they, too, end up in a place of torment.

Abraham replied, "They have Moses and the prophets; they should listen to them."

"No, father Abraham, but if someone from the dead goes to them, they will repent."

Abraham said, "If they do not listen to Moses and the prophets, neither will they be convinced even if someone rises from the dead." (Luke 16.19–31)

It's a parable. Hades, Abraham's bosom, Dives and Lazarus are fictions, but the moral lessons are not. How we treat others has long-term consequences. Social divisions are hard to overcome. There's no magical source for truth. The truth is all around and within us.

The right way to live is present in the books of Moses (the Torah) and the prophets—and in all the great religions and ethical systems or the world. The Golden Rule, for example, is universally acclaimed in multiple cultures. The truth is shouted from every mountaintop and along every byway. It's no secret. We have no excuse. We don't need someone to come back from the dead to tell us it's so.

Sadly, arguments over the facticity of the resurrection have become sideshows distracting many from the heart of Christianity: *Love one another as I have loved you.* And to tell you the truth, love of neighbor and care for the outsider were in the Torah long before Jesus made it his practice and mission.

To be fair, many people who believe in the bodily resurrection of Jesus practice kindness and charity. In fact, that single conviction empowers their morality. It makes them bold and fearless in the face of opposition and death.

So, if believing in the resurrection *as a literal fact* makes you a kinder person, I will not scoff or object. I will stand up and applaud. Still, I will not concede to your supernatural explanation or your claims for the superiority of Christianity. Nor will I allow belief in the literal resurrection be a litmus test of Christian faith.

## CHAPTER 21

# Is Jesus the Way, the Truth, and the Life?

The most quoted verse from the Bible by evangelicals is John 3.16: *For God so loved the world that he gave is only begotten son so that whoever believes in him will not perish but will have eternal life.*

The second is John 14.6: *I am the way and the truth and the life. No one comes to the Father except through me.*

Many Christians take that to mean that belief in Jesus is *the only way* to get to heaven when you die. I heard that over and over while growing up in a Baptist church. I never thought to question it. It seemed to be a solid fact. I believed it—even though I hadn't given much thought to what exactly "I am the way" meant. I guess I mostly thought Jesus was "the ticket" that got you in the door to heaven. No ticket. No entry.

Years later I'd learn of "the way of the Tao," the collected wisdom of the sixth century BCE Chinese philosopher Lao-tzu, and ask myself: Could "the way of Jesus" be similar? And then I had an epiphany. I saw what I'd missed. In the gospel of John, Jesus is an incarnation, an avatar, of love. So, connect that dot to this dot and EUREKA: Love, not Jesus, is *the way.*

DUH.

The word *love* appears fifty-seven times in the gospel of John—more than in all the other gospels combined. The prologue is: *In the beginning was the Word and the Word was with God and the Word was God.* (John 1.1) And that Word, we are told, was embodied in Jesus. And that "Word," as we'll see is "love."

But is the way of Jesus the way of love?

Come along and see for yourself.

The first time Jesus speaks in this gospel is to pose a question to two prospective disciples: "What are you looking for?"

"Where do you abide?" they asked.

"Come and see."

Which is to say: I won't tell you. You'll have to see for yourself.

Jesus did not take them to a house or to any one particular place. He took them on a journey to show them where he abides.

The first stop was a wedding in Cana. The wine ran out. Jesus turned one hundred and sixty gallons of water into wine. *Who does things like that?!* Well, Dionysus does. Dionysus, the most popular of the Greek gods, was a fountain of joy and ecstasy.

Is the way of Jesus like *that*?

What do you think?

A wine deficiency is not exactly a desperate human need—unless you are the wedding steward or the bride and groom. They were dejected. And then elated. We can't live on bread alone. We need wine. We need joy.

What is the way of Jesus?

That.

Exhilaration. Joy. In abundance.

*These things I have spoken to you, that my joy may remain in you, and that your joy may be full.* (John 13.11)

The journey continued.

As they went on their way, they saw Jesus heal a person who was dying, another who was blind, another who was lame. He also fed five thousand people and resurrected his friend Lazarus who had been dead and buried in a tomb for four days.

What is the way of Jesus?

That.

Healing. Feeding. Regeneration.

They arrived in Jerusalem and partook of a meal together, traditionally known as the Last Supper. After the meal Jesus knelt before his disciples, one by one, and washed their feet—a social ritual none of them was willing to perform. That was a job for servants or slaves, not for "important" people.

The supper scene concludes:

*A new command I give you: Love one another. As I have loved you, so you must love one another. By this everyone will know that you are my disciples, if you love one another.* (John 13.34)

Love *as.*

Love *as* I have loved you.

And how is that?

Stoop to serve.

Clearly, Jesus intended his movement to be known for compassion, not creeds, pomp, or conceit. Servanthood, not lordship. Kneeling, not strutting.

What is the way of Jesus?

That.

Serving. Compassion. Humility.

Jesus is the way, but he's also the light. In this gospel Jesus personifies many rich Jewish symbols.

*I am the light. I am the door. I am the bread. I am the vine. I am the good shepherd. I am the resurrection.*

The "way" is also a rich Jewish symbol for the path of life.

*The Lord watches over "the way" of the righteous; but "the way" of wicked will perish.* (Psalm 1)

"I am the way"—as the Torah is the way to a holy and wholesome life.

It took an epiphany (and some serious rereading of this gospel, verse by verse) for me to see the obvious: Love, not Jesus, is the way. Love, not Christianity, is the way. Love, not any religion or pious rituals, is the way, the truth, and the life.

The Tao of love.

Jesus doesn't abide in heaven. He abides in acts of kindness. He abides wherever love is needed, among the tormented, the hurting, and neglected. As it turns out, the way of Jesus is not a way out of this world. It's a certain way of being, a certain way of being in this world, a certain way of being in love with the earth and all creatures great and small.

That's how to abide in the "Father's house," the place where all are welcomed and loved.

Where do you abide?

Come and see.

# CHAPTER 22

# Is Jesus Coming Back?

*So when they had come together, they asked him, "Lord, is this the time when you will restore the kingdom to Israel?" He replied, "It is not for you to know the times or periods that the Father has set by his own authority. But you will receive power when the Holy Spirit has come upon you, and you will be my witnesses in Jerusalem, in all Judea and Samaria, and to the ends of the earth." When he had said this, as they were watching, he was lifted up, and a cloud took him out of their sight. While he was going and they were gazing up toward heaven, suddenly two men in white robes stood by them. They said, "Men of Galilee, why do you stand looking up toward heaven? This Jesus, who has been taken up from you into heaven, will come in the same way as you saw him go into heaven." (Acts 1.6–10)*

🍎 🍎 🍎

Is Jesus coming back?

No.

No more than Elijah is coming back.

Yet Jewish people keep setting an empty chair at the Passover Seder meal for Elijah every year. Just in case. But it's been three thousand years—and counting. Still no Elijah.

As we've seen, the gospels present Jesus in the guise of Elijah. Like Elijah, Jesus fed the hungry and raised the dead. Like Elijah, Jesus was raptured into heaven. Like Elijah, Jesus is coming back. Or so it is said.

Christians can set a chair for Jesus if they'd like. But he's not coming back.

Of course, we don't know everything. But we do know some things. And we're pretty sure no one's coming from heaven to save us. But we are not helpless.

We know we are resourceful, ingenious, and resilient. We know we are capable of great good and great evil. We know hubris brings us down; humility lifts us up. We know life is hard and often unfair.

We can fuss, fume, and fret. Or we can spend our days working together to make our shared home as beautiful, peaceful, just, whole, and sustainable as we possibly can. Perhaps God was at the beginning. Perhaps God will be at the end. We don't know. What we do know is: *We are here now.*

We know living for self alone is hell. Living for others is heaven.

Jesus said that. He doesn't have to come back to say it again. But if it takes an empty chair to remember what Jesus said, set an empty chair.

Yes, we're on our own.

But we are not alone.

We have each other.

And we have our stories.

🍎 🍎 🍎

# Conclusion

By now I hope you've taken the Bible off the pedestal or out of the trash can. I hope you've got the Bible on the table—open and ready to read again as though for the first time.

The Bible is a human product, a conglomeration of ancient Jewish works. Some beautiful, others drab. Some compelling, others appalling. The Bible is like any collection that could be assembled into one book from ancient Greek, Roman, Persian, Indian, or Chinese works. The Bible is also like a prospective collection of a hundred American books or films.

We can learn a great deal from such collections, but we would not call any of them THE WORD OF GOD. Nor should the Bible be called THE WORD OF GOD. It is not the supreme authority. We are free to take it into account, but we are by no means bound by it. If a church or individual wants to elevate it to a supreme position and be bound by it, so be it. That's on them, not on the rest of us. But such a church or individual should understand that they are deifying something human. And the Bible itself calls that "idolatry."

I see no harm in respecting the Bible as we do our venerable but flawed grandparents. They get some things right and some things wrong. But we can still respect them and learn from them. They are people of a certain time and place. We shouldn't hold that against them. We're smart enough to winnow the wheat from the chaff.

Yes, the Bible gets a lot of things wrong. After all, it's a human product from a distant time and culture. But it also gets some things right. And what it gets right isn't exactly new or startling. It's not exactly a revelation as much as an affirmation of what we already know. As the book of Ecclesiastes puts it: *There's nothing new under the sun.*

The parable of creation in Genesis 1 tells me life is hard. We all suffer. We find ourselves in darkness, chaos, everything under water time and time again. But the parable also tells me that things don't have to stay that way. It tells me I have agency. I'm not helpless. And that's the gospel long before the New Testament gospels were ever published.

The tower of Babel parable reminds us that together we can do great things. Yes, there are obstacles, but don't let them get us down. Look up. Keep building a new world.

And finally, we have the example of Jesus and many others to show us how to live rightly and fully in the present. Feed the hungry, heal the sick, soothe the tormented, welcome all to your table, practice compassion, renounce violence, love your enemies even if it kills you. Lose yourself, and you'll find yourself. Take up your cross. Die daily. Live fully.

Love is the way, the truth, and the life.

# Postlude

Three conjoined parables in the gospel of Luke encapsulate Jesus's vocation of mending the world, of bringing peace on earth, goodwill to all.

These parables are about finding something precious that was lost. A popular Christian interpretation of these parables is: *When we are lost (in sin), God finds us and returns us to where we belong. We are forgiven.* That's a theological lesson. But Amy-Jill Levine, distinguished Professor of New Testament and Jewish Studies at Hartford International University for Religion and Peace, helped me see that is not the only or the best interpretation.

I revisited those parables and saw something I hadn't seen before. I noticed—as though for the first time—the sneering question posed to Jesus by his critics. *Why do you eat with sinners?* Which is to say, why do you eat with deplorable people? Jesus replied by telling three parables.

These are three distinct parables, but they can be read as one act with three scenes. (Luke 15. See appendix for full text.)

In the first, a shepherd discovers that one of his one hundred sheep is lost. One hundred is a nice whole number. We feel something amiss with just ninety-nine on hand. The whole is incomplete.

The distraught shepherd leaves the ninety-nine behind and searches all through the night until he finds the missing one. He picks it up and carries it back to the fold. The whole is restored. The shepherd rejoices. The heavens rejoice. All is well. The diminished unit is whole again.

In the second, a woman discovers that one of her ten precious coins is lost. Ten is a nice whole number. We can feel something amiss with just nine on hand. The whole is incomplete.

The distraught woman searches high and low until she finds the coin. She picks it up and puts in back in her purse. The whole is restored. She rejoices. The heavens rejoice. All is well. The diminished unit is whole again.

Those two parables set the stage for the last and most telling of the three.

A father has two sons. He loses one.

As Levine points out, any Jewish story that begins with *A father had two sons* sets off alarms. Adam had two sons: Cain and Abel. Abraham had two sons: Ishmael and Isaac. Isaac had two sons: Esau and Jacob. All those stories are fraught with conflict, anger, and hatred.

In this third scene, the younger son demands his future inheritance. His father relents. The young man leaves his father and older brother at home and goes off to live it up in the world. He wastes it all and falls destitute, working on a pig farm. (Not a happy lot for a Jewish boy.)

The distraught father stands every day gazing toward the horizon, waiting and hoping for his son's return. Days, then weeks, then months go by.

Finally the son comes to his senses and goes home to ask forgiveness and to be treated as a mere servant of his father. He deserved nothing, but he would beg for mercy. Better a life of servitude than death, he reasons.

While he is still a long way off, his father sees him and runs to welcome him home. The father hears his son's confession but rejects his remedy ("make me a servant"). The father lifts the son up and drapes him in fine garments. The father rejoices.

(What a good man this father is!)

The father kills the fatted calf, throws a grand banquet for his lost-but-now-found son. The broken family is whole again. Let the heavens rejoice!

But, alas, not everyone in this family is happy.

The elder son is angry. And for good reason. His father had somehow forgotten to invite him to the banquet. One son was included, the other excluded.

(Things happen.)

The elder son hears the jubilation and comes toward the house. The father, realizing his oversight, rushes out to invite the neglected son in. Better late than never. But not in this case. The damage has been done.

The elder son vents his rage at his father over his mistreatment. It's Cain and Abel all over again. One son favored, the other unfavored.

Please come in, the father begs the older son.

The father returns to the party and leaves the door open.

And that's where the parable ends. The father and younger son are in the house. (In my father's house.) The older son is outside.

Seething.

Sin crouching at his door.

No one rejoices. The heavens are silent. We hold our breath. What will the older son do?

⚭ ⚭ ⚭

It's easy to pick up and restore a lost sheep to the fold. It's easy to pick up and restore a lost coin to a purse. It's not easy to mend the broken human family when any among us feels mistreated. It requires long and arduous work to make the broken world whole.

We can't force the world to live in peace. But we can open a door.

The arc of the universe doesn't inevitably bend toward justice. But it may if we work at it.

It may.

"Why do you eat with deplorable people?" the critics snapped at Jesus.

*Because my mission, like that of my great, great, great grandparents Abraham and Sarah, is to restore the broken human family to wholeness. To mend the world. To be a blessing. Somehow.*

May you make that your mission, too?

You may.

*Timshel.*

🍏 🍏 🍏

# Appendix

## Full Bible texts for Chapters 1, 6, 8–11, and Postlude

### CHAPTER 1. From Theism to Humanism

Exodus 3.1–15

Moses was keeping the flock of his father-in-law Jethro, the priest of Midian; he led his flock beyond the wilderness and came to Mount Horeb, the mountain of God. There the angel of the Lord appeared to him in a flame of fire out of a bush; he looked, and the bush was blazing, yet it was not consumed. Then Moses said, "I must turn aside and look at this great sight and see why the bush is not burned up." When the Lord saw that he had turned aside to see, God called to him out of the bush, "Moses, Moses!" And he said, "Here I am." Then he said, "Come no closer! Remove the sandals from your feet, for the place on which you are standing is holy ground." He said further, "I am the God of your father, the God of Abraham, the God of Isaac, and the God of Jacob." And Moses hid his face, for he was afraid to look at God.

Then the Lord said, "I have observed the misery of my people who are in Egypt; I have heard their cry on account of their taskmasters. Indeed, I know their sufferings, and I have come down to deliver them from the Egyptians and to bring them up out of that land to a good and spacious land, to a land flowing with milk and honey, to the country of the Canaanites, the Hittites, the Amorites, the Perizzites, the Hivites, and the Jebusites. The cry of the Israelites has now come to me; I have also seen how the Egyptians oppress them. Now go, I am sending you to Pharaoh to bring my people, the Israelites, out of Egypt."

But Moses said to God, "Who am I that I should go to Pharaoh and bring the Israelites out of Egypt?" He said, "I will be with you, and this shall be the sign for you that it is I who sent you: when you have brought the people out of Egypt, you shall serve God on this mountain."

Moses said to God, "If I come to the Israelites and say to them, 'The God of your ancestors has sent me to you,' and they ask me, 'What is his name?' what shall I say to them?"

God said to Moses, "I am who I am. [YHWH] Thus you shall say to the Israelites, 'I am [YHWH] has sent me to you.' Thus you shall say to the Israelites, 'The Lord, the God of your ancestors, the God of Abraham, the God of Isaac, and the God of Jacob, has sent me to you': This is my name forever, and this my title for all generations."

🍎 🍎 🍎

## Chapter 6. Lessons from the Parable of Creation

Genesis 1–2.3

When God began to create the heavens and the earth, the earth was complete chaos, and darkness covered the face of the deep, while a wind from God swept over the face of the waters. Then God said, "Let there be light," and there was light. And God saw that the light was good, and God separated the light from the darkness. God called the light Day, and the darkness he called Night. And there was evening and there was morning, the first day.

And God said, "Let there be a dome in the midst of the waters, and let it separate the waters from the waters." So God made the dome and separated the waters that were under the dome from the waters that were above the dome. And it was so. God called the dome Sky. And there was evening and there was morning, the second day.

And God said, "Let the waters under the sky be gathered together into one place, and let the dry land appear." And it was so. God called the dry land Earth, and the waters that were gathered together he called Seas. And God saw that it was good. Then God said, "Let the earth put forth vegetation: plants yielding seed and fruit trees of every kind on earth that bear fruit with the seed in it." And it was so. The earth brought forth vegetation: plants yielding seed of every kind and trees of every kind bearing fruit with the seed in it. And God saw that it was good. And there was evening and there was morning, the third day.

And God said, "Let there be lights in the dome of the sky to separate the day from the night, and let them be for signs and for seasons and for days and years, and let them be lights in the dome of the sky to give light upon the earth." And it was so. God made the two great lights—the greater light to rule the day and the lesser light to rule the night—and the stars. God set them in the dome of the sky to give light upon the earth, to rule over the day and over the night, and to separate the light from the darkness. And God saw that it was good. And there was evening and there was morning, the fourth day.

And God said, "Let the waters bring forth swarms of living creatures, and let birds fly above the earth across the dome of the sky." So God created the great sea monsters and every living creature that moves, of every kind, with which the waters swarm and every winged bird of every kind. And God saw that it was good. God blessed them, saying, "Be fruitful and multiply and fill the waters in the seas, and let birds multiply on the earth." And there was evening and there was morning, the fifth day.

And God said, "Let the earth bring forth living creatures of every kind: cattle and creeping things and wild animals of the earth of every kind." And it was so. God made the wild animals of the earth of every kind and the cattle of every kind and everything that creeps upon the ground of every kind. And God saw that it was good.

Then God said, "Let us make humans in our image, according to our likeness, and let them have dominion over the fish of the sea and over the birds of the air and over the cattle and over all the wild animals of the earth and over every creeping thing that creeps upon the earth."

> So God created humans in his image,
> in the image of God he created them;
> male and female he created them.

God blessed them, and God said to them, "Be fruitful and multiply and fill the earth and subdue it and have dominion over the fish of the sea and over the birds of the air and over every living thing that moves upon the earth." God said, "See, I have given you every plant yielding seed that is upon the face of all the earth and every tree with seed in its fruit; you shall have them for food. And to every beast of the earth and to every bird of the air and to everything that creeps on the earth, everything that has the breath of life, I have given every green plant for food." And it was so. God saw everything that he had made, and indeed, it was very good. And there was evening and there was morning, the sixth day.

Thus the heavens and the earth were finished and all their multitude. On the sixth day God finished the work that he had done, and he rested on the seventh day from all the work that he had done. So God blessed the seventh day and hallowed it, because on it God rested from all the work that he had done in creation.

🍎 🍎 🍎

## Chapter 8. Finding a Soulmate

Genesis 2.4–24

In the day that the Lord God made the earth and the heavens, when no plant of the field was yet in the earth and no vegetation of the field had yet sprung up—for the Lord God had not caused it to rain upon the earth, and there was no one to till the ground, but a stream would rise from the earth and water the whole face of the ground—then the Lord God formed man from the dust of the ground and breathed into his nostrils the breath of life, and the man became a living being. And the Lord God planted a garden in Eden, in the east, and there he put the man whom he had formed. Out of the ground the Lord God made to grow every tree that is pleasant to the sight and good for food, the tree of life also in the midst of the garden, and the tree of the knowledge of good and evil.

A river flows out of Eden to water the garden, and from there it divides and becomes four branches. The name of the first is Pishon; it is the one that flows around the whole land of Havilah, where there is gold, and the gold of that land is good; bdellium and onyx stone are there. The name of the second river is Gihon; it is the one that flows around the whole land of Cush. The name of the third river is Tigris, which flows east of Assyria. And the fourth river is the Euphrates.

The Lord God took the man and put him in the garden of Eden to till it and keep it. And the Lord God commanded the man, "You may freely eat of every tree of the garden, but of the tree of the knowledge of good and evil you shall not eat, for in the day that you eat of it you shall die."

Then the Lord God said, "It is not good that the man should be alone; I will make him a helper as his partner." So out of the ground the Lord God formed every animal of the field and every bird of the air and brought them to the man to see what he would call them, and whatever the man called every living creature, that was its name. The man gave names to all cattle and to the birds of the air and to every animal of the field, but for the man there was not found a helper as his partner. So the Lord God caused a deep sleep to fall upon the man, and he slept; then he took one of his ribs and closed up its place with flesh. And the rib that the Lord God had taken from the man he made into a woman and brought her to the man. Then the man said,

> *"This at last is bone of my bones*
> *and flesh of my flesh;*
> *this one shall be called Woman,*
> *for out of Man this one was taken."*

Therefore a man leaves his father and his mother and clings to his wife, and they become one flesh. And the man and his wife were both naked and were not ashamed.

🍎 🍎 🍎

## CHAPTER 9. Eve Is a Hero

Genesis 3.1–24

Now the serpent was more crafty than any other wild animal that the Lord God had made. He said to the woman, "Did God say, 'You shall not eat from any tree in the garden'?" The woman said to the serpent, "We may eat of the fruit of the trees in the garden, but God said, 'You shall not eat of the fruit of the tree that is in the middle of the garden, nor shall you touch it, or you shall die.'" But the serpent said to the woman, "You will not die, for God knows that when you eat of it your eyes will be opened, and you will be like God, knowing good and evil."

So when the woman saw that the tree was good for food and that it was a delight to the eyes and that the tree was to be desired to make one wise, she took of its fruit and ate, and she also gave some to her husband, who was with her, and he ate. Then the eyes of both were opened, and they knew that they were naked, and they sewed fig leaves together and made loincloths for themselves.

They heard the sound of the Lord God walking in the garden at the time of the evening breeze, and the man and his wife hid themselves from the presence of the Lord God among the trees of the garden. But the Lord God called to the man and said to him, "Where are you?" He said, "I heard the sound of you in the garden, and I was afraid, because I was naked, and I hid myself." He said, "Who told you that you were naked? Have you eaten from the tree of which I commanded you not to eat?" The man said, "The woman whom you gave to be with me, she gave me fruit from the tree, and I ate." Then the Lord God said to the woman, "What is this that you have done?" The woman said, "The serpent tricked me, and I ate." The Lord God said to the serpent,

*"Because you have done this,*
*cursed are you among all animals*
*and among all wild creatures;*
*upon your belly you shall go,*
*and dust you shall eat*
*all the days of your life.*

*I will put enmity between you and the woman*
*and between your offspring and hers;*
*he will strike your head,*
*and you will strike his heel."*

To the woman he said,

"I will make your pangs in childbirth exceedingly great;
in pain you shall bring forth children,
yet your desire shall be for your husband,
and he shall rule over you."

And to the man he said,

"Because you have listened to the voice of your wife
and have eaten of the tree
about which I commanded you,
You shall not eat of it,'
cursed is the ground because of you;
in toil you shall eat of it all the days of your life;

thorns and thistles it shall bring forth for you;
and you shall eat the plants of the field.

By the sweat of your face
you shall eat bread
until you return to the ground,
for out of it you were taken;
you are dust,
and to dust you shall return."

The man named his wife Eve because she was the mother of all living. And the Lord God made garments of skins for the man and for his wife and clothed them.

Then the Lord God said, "See, the humans have become like one of us, knowing good and evil, and now they might reach out their hands and take also from the tree of life and eat and live forever"—therefore the Lord God sent them forth from the garden of Eden, to till the ground from which they were taken. He drove out the humans, and at the east of the garden of Eden he placed the cherubim and a sword flaming and turning to guard the way to the tree of life.

🍏 🍏 🍏

# CHAPTER 10. The Birth of Violence

Genesis 4.1–24

Now the man knew his wife Eve, and she conceived and bore Cain, saying, "I have produced a man with the help of the Lord." Next she bore his brother Abel. Now Abel was a keeper of sheep, and Cain a tiller of the ground. In the course of time Cain brought to the Lord an offering of the fruit of the ground, and Abel for his part brought of the firstlings of his flock, their fat portions. And the Lord had regard for Abel and his offering, but for Cain and his offering he had no regard. So Cain was very angry, and his countenance fell. The Lord said to Cain, "Why are you angry, and why has your countenance fallen? If you do well, will you not be accepted? And if you do not do well, sin is lurking at the door; its desire is for you, but you must master it."

Cain said to his brother Abel, "Let us go out to the field." And when they were in the field, Cain rose up against his brother Abel and killed him. Then the Lord said to Cain, "Where is your brother Abel?" He said, "I do not know; am I my brother's keeper?" And the Lord said, "What have you done? Listen, your brother's blood is crying out to me from the ground! And now you are cursed from the ground, which has opened its mouth to receive your brother's blood from your hand. When you till the ground, it will no longer yield to you its strength; you will be a fugitive and a wanderer on the earth." Cain said to the Lord, "My punishment is greater than I can bear! Today you have driven me away from the soil, and I shall be hidden from your face; I shall be a fugitive and a wanderer on the earth, and anyone who meets me may kill me." Then the Lord said to him, "Not so! Whoever kills Cain will suffer a sevenfold vengeance." And the Lord put a mark on Cain, so that no one who came upon him would kill him. Then Cain went away from the presence of the Lord and settled in the land of Nod, east of Eden.

Cain knew his wife, and she conceived and bore Enoch, and he built a city and named it Enoch after his son Enoch. To Enoch was born Irad, and Irad was the father of Mehujael, and Mehujael the father of Methushael, and Methushael the father of Lamech. Lamech took two wives; the name of the one was Adah, and the name of the other Zillah. Adah bore Jabal; he was the ancestor of those who live in tents and have livestock. His brother's name was Jubal; he was the ancestor of all those who play the lyre and pipe. Zillah bore Tubal-cain, who made all kinds of bronze and iron tools. The sister of Tubal-cain was Naamah.

*Lamech said to his wives:*

*"Adah and Zillah, hear my voice;*
*you wives of Lamech, listen to what I say:*
*I have killed a man for wounding me,*
*a young man for striking me.*

*If Cain is avenged sevenfold,*
*truly Lamech seventy-sevenfold."*

🍎 🍎 🍎

## CHAPTER 11. Violence Procreates

Genesis 6–9 (slightly abridged)

When people began to multiply on the face of the ground, and daughters were born to them, the sons of God saw that they were fair, and they took wives for themselves of all that they chose. Then the Lord said, "My spirit shall not abide in mortals forever, for they are flesh; their days shall be one hundred twenty years."

The Lord saw that the wickedness of humans was great in the earth and that every inclination of the thoughts of their hearts was only evil continually. And the Lord was sorry that he had made humans on the earth, and it grieved him to his heart. So the Lord said, "I will blot out from the earth the humans I have created— people together with animals and creeping things and birds of the air—for I am sorry that I have made them." But Noah found favor in the sight of the Lord.

Now the earth was corrupt in God's sight, and the earth was filled with violence. And God saw that the earth was corrupt, for all flesh had corrupted its ways upon the earth. And God said to Noah, "I have determined to make an end of all flesh, for the earth is filled with violence because of them; now I am going to destroy them along with the earth. Make yourself an ark of cypress wood; make rooms in the ark, and cover it inside and out with pitch. This is how you are to make it: the length of the ark three hundred cubits, its width fifty cubits, and its height thirty cubits. Make a roof for the ark, and finish it to a cubit above, and put the door of the ark in its side; make it with lower, second, and third decks. For my part, I am going to bring a flood of waters on the earth, to destroy from under heaven all flesh in which is the breath of life; everything that is on the earth shall die. But I will establish my covenant with you, and you shall come into the ark, you, your sons, your wife, and your sons' wives with you. And of every living thing, of all flesh, you shall bring two of every kind into the ark, to keep them alive with you; they shall be male and female. Of the birds according to their kinds and of the animals according to their kinds, of every creeping thing of the ground according to its kind, two of every kind shall come in to you, to keep them alive. Also take with you every kind of food that is eaten, and store it up, and it shall serve as food for you and for them." Noah did this; he did all that God commanded him.

Then the Lord said to Noah, "Go into the ark, you and all your household, for I have seen that you alone are righteous before me in this generation. Take with you seven pairs of all clean animals, the male and its mate; and a pair of the animals that are not clean, the male and its mate; and seven pairs of the birds of the air also, male and female, to keep their kind alive on the face of all the earth. For in seven days I will send rain on the earth for forty days and forty nights, and every living thing that I have made I will blot out from the face of the ground." And Noah did all that the Lord had commanded him.

Noah was six hundred years old when the flood of waters came on the earth. And Noah with his sons and his wife and his sons' wives went into the ark to escape the waters of the flood. And after seven days the waters of the flood came on the earth.

In the six hundredth year of Noah's life, in the second month, on the seventeenth day of the month, on that day all the fountains of the great deep burst forth, and the windows of the heavens were opened. The rain fell on the earth forty days and forty nights.

The waters swelled so mightily on the earth that all the high mountains under the whole heaven were covered; the waters swelled above the mountains, covering them fifteen cubits deep.

And all flesh died that moved on the earth, birds, domestic animals, wild animals, all swarming creatures that swarm on the earth, and all human beings; everything on dry land in whose nostrils was the breath of life died. He blotted out every living thing that was on the face of the ground, human beings and animals and creeping things and birds of the air; they were blotted out from the earth. Only Noah was left and those with him in the ark. And the waters swelled on the earth for one hundred fifty days.

But God remembered Noah and all the wild animals and all the domestic animals that were with him in the ark. And God made a wind blow over the earth, and the waters subsided; the fountains of the deep and the windows of the heavens were closed, the rain from the heavens was restrained, and the waters gradually receded from the earth. At the end of one hundred fifty days the waters had abated, and in the seventh month, on the seventeenth day of the month, the ark came to rest on the mountains of Ararat. The waters continued to abate until the tenth month; in the tenth month, on the first day of the month, the tops of the mountains appeared.

At the end of forty days Noah opened the window of the ark that he had made and sent out the raven, and it went to and fro until the waters were dried up from the earth. Then he sent out the dove from him to see if the waters had subsided from the face of the ground, but the dove found no place to set its foot, and it returned to him to the ark, for the waters were still on the face of the whole earth. So he put out his hand and took it and brought it into the ark with him. He waited another seven days, and again he sent out the dove from the ark, and the dove came back to him in the evening, and there in its beak was a freshly plucked olive leaf; so Noah knew that the waters had subsided from the earth. Then he waited another seven days and sent out the dove, and it did not return to him any more.

In the six hundred and first year, in the first month, on the first day of the month, the waters were dried up from the earth, and Noah removed the covering of the ark and looked and saw that the face of the ground was drying. In the second month, on the twenty-seventh day of the month, the earth was dry. Then God said to Noah, "Go out of the ark, you and your wife and your sons and your sons' wives with you. Bring out with you every living thing that is with you of all flesh—birds and animals and every creeping thing that creeps on the earth—so that they may abound on the earth and be fruitful and multiply on the earth." So Noah went out with his sons and his wife and his sons' wives. And every animal, every creeping thing, and every bird, everything that moves on the earth, went out of the ark by families.

Then Noah built an altar to the Lord and took of every clean animal and of every clean bird and offered burnt offerings on the altar. And when the Lord smelled the pleasing odor, the Lord said in his heart, "I will never again curse the ground because of humans, for the inclination of the human heart is evil from youth; nor will I ever again destroy every living creature as I have done.

> As long as the earth endures,
> seedtime and harvest, cold and heat,
> summer and winter, day and night
> shall not cease."

God blessed Noah and his sons and said to them, "Be fruitful and multiply and fill the earth. The fear and dread of you shall rest on every animal of the earth and on every bird of the air, on everything that creeps on the ground and on all the fish of the sea; into your hand they are delivered. Every moving thing that lives shall be food for you, and just as I gave you the green plants, I give you everything. Only, you shall not eat flesh with its life, that is, its blood. For your own lifeblood I will surely require a reckoning: from every animal I will require it and from human beings, each one for the blood of another, I will require a reckoning for human life.

> Whoever sheds the blood of a human,
> by a human shall that person's blood be shed,
> for in his own image
> God made humans.

"And you, be fruitful and multiply, abound on the earth and have dominion over it."

Then God said to Noah and to his sons with him, "As for me, I am establishing my covenant with you and your descendants after you and with every living creature that is with you, the birds, the domestic animals, and every animal of the earth with you, as many as came out of the ark. I establish my covenant with you, that never again shall all flesh be cut off by the waters of a flood, and never again shall there be a flood to destroy the earth." God said, "This is the sign of the covenant that I make between me and you and every living creature that is with you, for all future generations: I have set my bow in the clouds, and it shall be a sign of the covenant between me and the earth."

The sons of Noah who went out of the ark were Shem, Ham, and Japheth. Ham was the father of Canaan. These three were the sons of Noah, and from these the whole earth was peopled.

Noah, a man of the soil, was the first to plant a vineyard. He drank some of the wine and became drunk, and he lay uncovered in his tent. And Ham, the father of Canaan, saw the nakedness of his father and told his two brothers outside. Then Shem and Japheth took a garment, laid it on both their shoulders, and walked backward and covered the nakedness of their father; their faces were turned away, and they did not see their father's nakedness. When Noah awoke from his wine and knew what his youngest son had done to him, he said,

> *"Cursed be Canaan;*
> *lowest of slaves shall he be to his brothers."*

*He also said,*

> *"Blessed by the Lord my God be Shem,*
> *and let Canaan be his slave.*

> *May God make space for Japheth,*
> *and let him live in the tents of Shem,*
> *and let Canaan be his slave."*

After the flood Noah lived three hundred fifty years. All the days of Noah were nine hundred fifty years, and he died.

🍎 🍎 🍎

## POSTLUDE

Luke 15.1–32

Now all the tax collectors and sinners were coming near to listen to him. And the Pharisees and the scribes were grumbling and saying, "This fellow welcomes sinners and eats with them."

So he told them this parable: "Which one of you, having a hundred sheep and losing one of them, does not leave the ninety-nine in the wilderness and go after the one that is lost until he finds it? And when he has found it, he lays it on his shoulders and rejoices. And when he comes home, he calls together his friends and neighbors, saying to them, 'Rejoice with me, for I have found my lost sheep.' Just so, I tell you, there will be more joy in heaven over one sinner who repents than over ninety-nine righteous persons who need no repentance.

"Or what woman having ten silver coins, if she loses one of them, does not light a lamp, sweep the house, and search carefully until she finds it? And when she has found it, she calls together her friends and neighbors, saying, 'Rejoice with me, for I have found the coin that I had lost.' Just so, I tell you, there is joy in the presence of the angels of God over one sinner who repents."

Then Jesus said, "There was a man who had two sons. The younger of them said to his father, 'Father, give me the share of the wealth that will belong to me.' So he divided his assets between them. A few days later the younger son gathered all he had and traveled to a distant region, and there he squandered his wealth in dissolute living. When he had spent everything, a severe famine took place throughout that region, and he began to be in need. So he went and hired himself out to one of the citizens of that region, who sent him to his fields to feed the pigs. He would gladly have filled his stomach with the pods that the pigs were eating, and no one gave him anything. But when he came to his senses he said, 'How many of my father's hired hands have bread enough and to spare, but here I am dying of hunger! I will get up and go to my father, and I will say to him, "Father, I have sinned against heaven and before you; I am no longer worthy to be called your son; treat me like one of your hired hands." So he set off and went to his father. But while he was still far off, his father saw him and was filled with compassion; he ran and put his arms around him and kissed him. Then the son said to him, 'Father, I have sinned against heaven and before you; I am no longer worthy to be called your son.' But the father said to his slaves, 'Quickly, bring out a robe—the best one—and put it on him; put a ring on his finger and sandals on his feet. And get the fatted calf and kill it, and let us eat and celebrate, for this son of mine was dead and is alive again; he was lost and is found!' And they began to celebrate.

"Now his elder son was in the field, and as he came and approached the house, he heard music and dancing. He called one of the slaves and asked what was going on. He replied, 'Your brother has come, and your father has killed the fatted calf because he has got him back safe and sound.' Then he became angry and refused to go in. His father came out and began to plead with him. But he answered his father, 'Listen! For all these years I have been working like a slave for you, and I have never disobeyed your command, yet you have never given me even a young goat so that I might celebrate with my friends. But when this son of yours came back, who has devoured your assets with prostitutes, you killed the fatted calf for him!' Then the father said to him, 'Son, you are always with me, and all that is mine is yours. But we had to celebrate and rejoice, because this brother of yours was dead and has come to life; he was lost and has been found.' "

# Suggested Reading

*The Bible: A Biography*, by Karen Armstrong. Grove Press, 2008.

*A History of the Bible: The Book and Its Faiths*, by John Barton. Penguin Books, 2020.

*Reading the Bible Again for the First Time: Taking the Bible Seriously but Not Literally*, by Marcus J. Borg. HarperOne, 2002.

*The Seven Pillars of Creation: The Bible, Science, and the Ecology of Wonder*, by William P. Brown. Oxford University Press, 2010.

*Rabbi Jesus: An Intimate Biography*, by Bruce Chilton. Random House, 2002.

*Jesus: A Revolutionary Biography*, by John Dominic Crossan. HarperOne, 1994.

*How Jesus Became God: The Exaltation of a Jewish Preacher from Galilee*, by Bart Ehrman. HarperOne, 2014.

*Misquoting Jesus: The Story Behind Who Changed the Bible and Why*, by Bart Ehrman. HarperOne, 2005.

*When Christians Were Jews: The First Generation*, by Paula Fredriksen. Yale University Press, 2018.

*The Misunderstood Jew: The Church and the Scandal of the Jewish Jesus*, by Amy-Jill Levine. HarperOne, 2007.

*America's Book: The Rise and Decline of a Bible Civilization, 1794–1911*, by Mark Noll. Oxford University Press, 2022.

*Hopeful Realism: Reclaiming the Poetry of Theology*, by Douglas F. Ottati. Wipf and Stock, 2009.

*Adam, Eve, and the Serpent*, by Elaine Pagels. Vintage, 1989.

*Jesus and Nonviolence: A Third Way*, by Walter Wink. Fortress Press, 2003.

🍏 🍏 🍏

# About the Author

Randall Tremba was born and raised in Youngstown, Ohio. He took a bachelor of arts in philosophy at Wheaton College, a master of divinity at Fuller Theological Seminary, and a doctor of ministry at Princeton Seminary. He was installed as minister of Shepherdstown (WV) Presbyterian Church in July 1976. Forty-one years later he retired. In between, he married Paula Egan, became a parent and a grandparent, founded the Rumsey Radio Hour, and cofounded the Shepherdstown *Good News Paper* with Ed Zahniser. He has published two books: *Let Love Arise* (2019) and *80 Dispatches from the Devil's Domain* (2021). He posts a dispatch Sunday mornings from his blog, www.thedevilsgift.com.